BRUTALISM

POST-WAR BRITISH ARCHITECTURE

SECOND EDITION

BRUTALISM

POST-WAR BRITISH ARCHITECTURE

SECOND EDITION

ALEXANDER CLEMENT

THE CROWOOD PRESS

First published in 2011 by
The Crowood Press Ltd
Ramsbury, Marlborough
Wiltshire SN8 2HR

www.crowood.com

Revised edition 2018

British Library Cataloguing-in-Publication Data
A catalogue record for this book is available from the British Library.

ISBN 978 1 78500 423 0

Acknowledgements
In the researching and writing of this book I would like to acknowledge the help and support of the following people: Andrea and Theo Clement, Jimmy Jaques, Stephen Clarke, Christine Otterwill and Kevin McGimpsey. I would also like to extend grateful thanks to Kendal Goode and Chief Superintendent Purdie of the North Wales Police, Sasha Ricketts, Terry Brown and Mick Farrell from GMW Architects, Sue Foster at Building Design Magazine, Pam Afghan at the Ministry of Justice, Karen Robinson at the Trades Union Congress, Mark Hansford and Sally Harper at The Economist Newspaper Ltd, Nick Saffell at the Cambridge University Office of Media Relations, Delwyn Evans at Flintshire County Council and Ather Mirza at the Leicester University Press and Corporate Communications Office.

Photography Credits
The images in this book have been taken by the author, with the exception of the following for which grateful thanks go to: Iqbal Alaam (the Chapel at Churchill College, Cambridge and Nottingham Playhouse), Darren Ashley (Chapter Hall, Truro Cathedral), Colin Brooks (Engineering Building, Charles Wilson Building and Attenborough Tower, Leicester University), Adam Brown at Durham University (Dunelm House, Durham), Elliott Brown (Birmingham Central Library), Steve Cadman (Cripps Building, Cambridge), Stephen Clarke (Trinity Car Park, Gateshead), Tim Eccleston (Coventry Cathedral), Johnathan Falkingham at Urban Splash (Park Hill Housing, Sheffield), Roger and Jane Kelly (Bernat Klein Studio), Adam Kerfoot-Roberts (Halifax Building), David Martyn (Clifton Roman Catholic Cathedral), Aiden McMichael (Ulster Museum Extension), Ste Passant (Preston Bus Station), Debbie Soon (New Court, Cambridge). Images of the University of East Anglia (UEA) were provided by courtesy of the University.

Typeset and designed by D & N Publishing, Baydon, Wiltshire.

Printed and bound in India by Parksons Graphics

Contents

Preface to the Second Edition

When I began writing the first edition of *Brutalism* at the beginning of 2009, the subject was something of a niche interest. Indeed, the one question I was asked most frequently by those people who generously gave their time and help to the project was 'Why on earth do you want to write about that?' Brutalism was a term almost unknown in its meaning and context other than by architects and architectural historians. Hardly anyone knew what I was talking about and why 'big ugly concrete buildings' might be a subject worth writing about. Today, though, the scene is very different. Brutalism as an interest has taken on a life of its own, with a host of books, publications, social media interest groups, documentaries, seminars, blogs and even guided tours devoted to it. This is deeply heartening to someone who took a small risk in standing in defence of preserving and celebrating Brutalist buildings. So widespread has the interest in post-war Modernist architecture become that my original book, released in 2011, needed revision to bring it closer to the exacting standards now set in the genre.

As key examples of Brutalism find themselves still threatened by, and even sadly suffering, demolition, there has been a return to an apparent polarity in our understanding of the term. This polarity was observed by Reyner Banham as early as 1955, when he wrote in the *Architectural Review* about the dichotomy between 'ethic and aesthetic'. Although the debate may be slightly removed from that today, Brutalism seems to mean different things to different people. However, it is the aesthetic side of things that often holds court, much above the consideration of materials and design espoused by Alison and Peter Smithson. To most observers and enthusiasts today, it means heavily massed rough-cast concrete, asymmetrical chunky forms and monumental megastructures. But there is another Brutalism, one that is often lost amid the clamour of surface appearances. The Brutalism of the Smithsons and Team 10 was about using high-quality materials left 'as found', exposed to speak for themselves, where the structure is clearly visible from the outside and where these factors work in concert to form a memorable image. There are some exceptional examples of Brutalism where concrete is not the primary facing material, but nevertheless the beating heart of the structure is purely Brutalist.

My book has, I will be the first to admit, been eclipsed by more recent publications on the subject, and so my small contribution to the genre now stands as a step towards the greater understanding and support Brutalism currently enjoys. It was never intended to be a masterwork of forensic academic research, and neither was it a comprehensive catalogue of every Brutalist building in the United Kingdom. Many of the chosen examples, far from being random, were earmarked for special attention by the Royal Institute of British Architects (RIBA) when the organisation chronicled British post-war building back in the 1980s. Some won awards and accolades at the time, in spite of later public derision. This second edition of *Brutalism* affords greater attention to buildings and schemes that could not be included in the first edition, as well as enhanced illustrations. I hope the reader finds these to be welcome improvements.

Alexander Clement, 2017

Introduction

The term 'Brutalism', when used to describe a specific type of Modernist architecture, has an uncertain origin. The Swedish architect Hans Asplund, writing in the *Architectural Review* in 1956, suggested that he coined the phrase in 1950 when describing the work of his colleagues Bengt Edman and Lennart Holm. The term then emigrated with them to Britain, where it was taken up by a select group of young up-and-coming architects. The first time the term was written down, though, was by Alison Smithson in 1952 in documenting a design for a new private house in Chelsea. By 1966 the word was fixed in the public and industry consciousness with the publication of Reyner Banham's book *The New Brutalism: Ethic or Aesthetic.*

What Brutalism describes is an uncompromisingly modern form of architecture which appeared and developed mainly in Europe between approximately 1945 and 1975. It is distinctive, arresting, exciting and, at the same time, like almost no other form of architecture before it, able to generate extreme emotions and heated debate. The use of modern materials predominates: concrete, steel and glass, although other more traditional ones were used in this period too, such as marble, stone and brick, but in a distinctively modern way. It is characterized by large, sometimes monumental, forms brought together in a unified whole with heavy, often asymmetrical proportions. Where concrete was used it was usually unadorned and rough-cast, adding to its unfortunate reputation for evoking a bleak dystopian future.

What begins to emerge to anyone studying this period is that there are three distinct phases of British post-war Modernism. I would identify these as, first, the 'Early' period which spanned approximately 1945 to 1960. During this time most buildings were essentially versions of the pre-war International Style or of Scandinavian influence. Then between around 1960 and 1975 came the 'Massive' period where the use of rough-cast concrete in chunky, asymmetrical forms predominated. Lastly, between 1975 and 1985 was what could be termed the 'Transitional' period where we find the use of brick combined with concrete and less monumental forms, stepping towards what would become the Neo-vernacular.

Now that the age of Brutalism is a comfortable thirty years in the past, there is an opportunity to look back at the way this style evolved in Britain, shaping the urban landscape and imprinting its character on our geography. Like few other countries, Britain possessed the optimum political and cultural environment following the Second World War for Modernist architecture to emerge from the shadows and become part of the mainstream. How it was that Brutalism became the style of choice this book aims to explore, studying its several forms and the functions modernist architecture was put to, looking at specific examples in context. In conclusion, the book will suggest what future there is for Brutalism in Britain – how the existing examples from the immediate post-war period will survive and share our spaces with new buildings both modern and vernacular and how Brutalism has found its way into the vocabulary of twenty-first-century buildings.

CONCRETE

Concrete is a building material comprising cement with other aggregate mixes, such as limestone, gravel and granite, which is mixed with sand and water. Once mixed, a chemical reaction takes place binding the whole together to form a dense, hard-wearing and strong material. Concrete was used by the Romans, indeed, the name is derived from the Latin *concretus*, meaning condensed or clotted, and a notable example of its use can be found at the Pantheon in Rome (*c*.AD126), with its massive dome. The material was almost entirely absent from world architecture until it was revived in France in the late eighteenth century and known as *béton*. It was here during the nineteenth century that architects began to experiment with reinforcing concrete, using iron to form floors, beams and columns. Its wider use in Europe and the United States during the late nineteenth and into the twentieth century allowed other methods to develop which became important to its use as an exposed building material in the Brutalist period, some of which are detailed here.

Reinforced Concrete

As a building material, concrete is brittle on its own and lacks structural integrity under stress when used in supporting work. Reinforcement with metal, usually with iron or steel rods, provided exactly the tensile strength needed for concrete to form large sections which could carry heavy weights.

Pre-cast Concrete

Concrete-constructed buildings will frequently use elements which have been pre-cast off-site. This is done by using moulds into which the concrete mixture is poured and then allowed to cure under controlled conditions. The pre-cast pieces are then taken to the construction site to be fitted into place. Commonly pre-cast elements are floor and wall slabs or exterior cladding.

In situ Concrete

The alternative to using pre-cast elements is to construct the moulds on-site and pour in the concrete to cure in position. This method is generally used for larger, more monumental structures and elements. The moulds are usually made of wood panels or planks, known as shuttering, with metal reinforcing rods and lattices positioned ready. Once dry, the exterior mould is dismantled, leaving the concrete sections in place. These are usually fettled and polished to remove the casting seams left where panel sections were joined. During the Brutalist period this was one of the most common forms of construction and a characteristic of some buildings, such as Denys Lasdun's National Theatre, left the concrete unpolished showing the casting seams on the exterior surfaces. This rough and unadorned form of concrete was termed by French architect Le Corbusier as *béton brut*.

Prestressed Concrete

Even with metal reinforcing, some concrete building elements, such as beams to support floor and ceiling slabs, may fracture under the stresses imposed on them. Prestressing is a technique used to prevent this. The normal method for treating a section is to stretch the metal reinforcing rods while the concrete is cast and then, once the mixture has cured, to release the rods, allowing the concrete to withstand load-bearing stresses when put into position.

Post-tensioned Concrete

This comes in two forms, bonded and unbonded, which result from the processes used with *in situ* casting. In bonded post-tensioning, the concrete is poured into a mould around steel cable tendons and allowed to cure. Once the concrete has cured, the cables are tensioned by using hydraulic jacks before being wedged into position and sealed to prevent corrosion. Unbonded post-tensioning is a similar process but here the steel cables are covered with a polythene sheath to allow them to move freely within the concrete. While the stress from tensioning is still transferred to the concrete, unbonded tendons can be detensioned, should the concrete section need to be repaired. Post-tensioning is generally used in situations where a structure requires stability against ground movement.

Chapter 1

Historical Context

To understand fully the development of Brutalism in Britain, we must first look at the genesis of Modernist architecture in the twentieth century. Probably the single most significant influential force in the development of Modernist design and architecture was the Industrial Revolution. This not only provided new materials and construction methods but also heralded a new age, the machine age, and a rapidly changing socio-economic landscape as the nineteenth century drew to a close.

As 1900 approached, there was a groundswell of interest, particularly in Europe, in cultivating a style of design and architecture which embraced the spirit of the age. Many practitioners felt that the best way to find this style would be to break completely with tradition, to move away from historicist ornamentation. To the growing army of 'modernists', the notion of dressing up a factory or an office block to look like a Greek temple or Venetian Renaissance palazzo was an absurdity.

Beginnings

Approaches to this problem of style varied dramatically in the early years of the twentieth century and it was not for over two decades that something resembling a cohesive Modern Movement emerged. In Spain Antoni Gaudi explored organic forms in a uniquely Expressionistic way. Organic forms were also prominent in France around the turn of the century, but applied differently in the Art Nouveau style, exemplified by the work of Victor Horta and Hector Guimard. But to some practitioners the work of Horta and his ilk was considered too ostentatious and dependent on ornamentation. A signal to an alternative direction in architecture came in the work of Auguste Perret from around 1905 onwards, who used reinforced concrete structures which were entirely visible, reducing historical ornament to a minimum so that the exterior could reflect the inner structure rather than hiding it.

This notion of stripping away ornament to allow the structure of a building to be seen and, indeed, celebrated, became a core theme among architects throughout Europe by the 1920s. In Germany the designer Peter Behrens espoused the notion of finding beauty in objects that reflected their function without unnecessary embellishment. This sense of design integrity was initially inspired by the British Arts and Crafts Movement and the teachings of William Morris. Behrens's most celebrated work was produced as architect and consultant for the A.E.G. Company, for whom he designed the Turbine Factory in Berlin (1909) which embodied his philosophy of form following function.

Between the wars Germany was a hotbed of *avant-gardism,* fuelled by the liberal Weimar Republic, which meant that new concepts of style in design and architecture were allowed to flourish. One particular nerve centre for such work was the Bauhaus design school, founded in 1919, when the Grand Ducal School of Arts

LE CORBUSIER

The French architect and designer Le Corbusier is regarded as one of the fathers of Modernism and is arguably the father of Brutalism. Born Charles-Édouard Jeanneret-Gris in 1887 at the French-Swiss town of La Chaux-de-Fonds, he took his pseudonym from a maternal ancestor *Le Corbesier* which he modified into *Le Corbusier*, suggesting crow-like qualities, which he used in his early writings and later as architect and town planner. He studied under Charles l'Eplattenier at the local art school and it was this teacher who persuaded him to abandon painting and take up architecture.

Jeanneret toured Europe in the early 1900s, coming into contact with designers such as Josef Hoffman, Frantz Jourdain and Eugene Grasset, the last of whom introduced him to the Perret brothers. In 1908–09 Jeanneret worked at the Atelier Perret, learning about the principles of reinforced concrete which the brothers had begun to use extensively in their designs. Through this period he began to leave behind the organic formalism of his art-school days and develop theories about architecture which leant strongly towards functionalism. Also of influence was a period in the office of the German industrial designer Peter Behrens, but his journey into Asia Minor and Greece in 1911 brought him in contact with architecture that had a simple geometry and which, with its pale, stuccoed facades, reflected the dazzling light of the region. He also found in the Parthenon at Athens a purity of form and spirit that would greatly influence his later work.

The two key elements that Le Corbusier brought to his own work over the next ten years or so were the 'Dom-ino' system and his 'five points' of new architecture, both of which would permeate his work through to the post-war period. The Dom-ino system (derived from the Latin *Domus* meaning house and a contraction of innovation) was designed to allow modular dwellings to be simply built and expanded and was based on three floor slabs supported on six columns, with stairs attached at one end to give access to each floor. This led towards his developing the five points of new architecture, which Le Corbusier held as the basic principles of building in the modern age, a thesis that he wrote in 1925 and published in 1927. They were:

■ Pilotis, raising the main structure above the ground supported by narrow columns;
■ Free facade, setting no restriction on the exterior surfaces;
■ Free plan, the structure allowing complete freedom from interior supporting walls;
■ Ribbon windows, which would provide uninterrupted views from inside;
■ Roof garden, creating a usable exterior space to replace the ground taken up by the building's footprint.

and Crafts and the Weimar Academy of Fine Arts merged. The School's new director Walter Gropius reinvigorated the institution, designing its new buildings and recruiting a new wave of faculty tutors, including László Moholy-Nagy, Paul Klee and Wassily Kandinsky, who were all to become leading lights of the Modern Movement.

The International Style

What developed in Europe, almost independently, was a new style of architecture which eschewed ornament and embraced the machine age, using materials such as steel, glass and concrete in new ways and setting aside the conventions of the past. Modernist buildings had

The two buildings which exemplified these theories and gave life to Le Corbusier's imagination were his *Pavillon de l'Esprit Nouveau* of 1925, built for the Paris Exposition of the same year, and the Villa Savoye of 1931. The latter, which still stands, was built at Poissy near Paris and has come to symbolize the International Style and the first phase of truly modern architecture.

In the immediate post-war period Le Corbusier's architecture took a new direction aesthetically, although it still embodied the principles developed during the previous twenty-five years. The first flowering of this new style came in the form of a project he was commissioned to build in Marseille as part of a scheme to address an acute housing shortage at the time. The *Unité d'Habitation* (1947–52) was a study in modular housing as well as social engineering with its combination of dwellings, shops and recreational facilities. But aesthetically it was a departure from the stuccoed purity of his pre-war houses. Here the concrete structure was left unadorned and rough-cast, the massing of volumes was heavy, chunky and brutal. It was, one might argue, the birth of Brutalism. The other key structures at this time were the Jaoul houses at Neiully-sur-Seine (1951–55), with the combination of brick and *béton brut* concrete in distinctive arched forms, which would resonate throughout British Brutalism in the coming decades. Structures that followed, including his monastery at La Tourette and his scheme for the parliament buildings at Chandigarh in India, confirmed the new direction in modern architecture that would influence the pioneers of Brutalism in Britain and elsewhere.

Regarded as the archetypal International Style villa, Le Corbusier's Villa Savoye at Poissy in France, 1931, encapsulated the architect's 'five points' of modern architecture.

completely free plans often with no internal load-bearing walls, which also allowed for large expanses of glass, cantilevered floors, smooth blank exterior elevations and flat roofs, which could house terraces and sun decks.

Much of the work of architects such as Gropius in Germany, Le Corbusier in France and J.J.P. Oud in Holland seemed to coincide stylistically and philosophically in the 1920s. This new wave became known as the International Style, after an exhibition of the same name organized by Alfred Barr, Henry-Russell Hitchcock and Phillip Johnson at the Museum of Modern Art in New York, in 1932. The exhibition catalogue sought to group examples of modern architecture of the day stylistically, although it was later criticized for omitting examples that did not conform to their criteria. What the exhibition achieved, however, was a holistic appreciation of the new style, identifying a common language between architects all over the world.

Two other events should also be identified as decisive to the development of this new architectural vocabulary: the *Weissenhoff Siedlung* exhibition in Stuttgart, 1927, and the formation of the *Congrès Internationaux d'Architecture Moderne* (CIAM) in the following year.

The Weissenhoff estate comprised a collection of twenty-one buildings which formed the *Deutsche Werkbund* exhibition of 1927. Organized and administrated by Ludwig Mies van der Rohe, the exhibition brought together sixteen architects from Germany, Holland and France to produce individual houses and apartment dwellings for working-class people. What is significant about the exhibition is the congruous style of the buildings: free plans, ribbon windows, pilotis, interlocking spaces and rendered exteriors devoid of historical ornamentation. At Weissenhoff, the work of European architects to develop a new style solidified, although a great deal still had to be done to reconcile economic and cultural barriers.

A further step towards a cohesive Modern Movement in architecture came in 1928 with the formation of the CIAM. The inaugural meeting was organized by Le Corbusier at the Chateau de la Sarraz in Switzerland and included twenty-eight European architects. The group not only identified the principles of the movement but sought also to act as a political collective, using urban planning to improve the world.

Trends in North America

It is important also to look at the development of modern architecture in North America, which was to have a direct impact on what would happen in Britain after the Second World War. Like Britain during the first half of the twentieth century, America developed the materials and the technology to produce truly modern buildings but lacked the political will, cultural need or cohesive *avant-garde* to advance with a new vocabulary as happened in Europe. Initially, the new materials and technologies were used to solve the problems of space in crowded urban centres by extending upwards. While these technically modern buildings pushed the boundaries of engineering and began changing the skylines of cities such as Chicago and New York, the first examples were clad in traditional materials and historical ornament.

One North American architect did break from these traditions, although not in quite the same way as his European contemporaries. Frank Lloyd Wright (1869–1959) took vernacular architecture and reinterpreted it in an increasingly stylized way. Indeed, much of his work during the early 1900s had more in common with that of the Vienna Secession (and particularly with interior detail) and with Charles Rennie Mackintosh than with the International Style. In spite of this, though, Wright's work was noticed from Europe and influenced both Oud and Gropius. Through the inter-war period Wright brought to his projects a monumentality of style which would later play a key role in the development of Brutalism.

Trends in Britain

The British architectural scene between 1900 and 1930 was, by contrast, resoundingly historicist. Like North America, Britain enjoyed a period of complacency while Victoria's empire remained pre-eminent, which meant that there was no cultural or political impetus to fuel the development of a new style in architecture, but, as in America, materials and techniques did develop and so under the traditional skin of many late nineteenth-century buildings there was something decidedly modern going on.

Reinforced concrete can be seen as early as 1897 at Weavers Mill in Swansea, designed by the French émigré Louis Gustave Mouchel. Steel structures emerged in the early 1900s, perhaps the most celebrated example being Daniel Burnham's building for the Selfridge department store on Oxford Street in London, of 1910. Here the essentially Neo-classical facade covered a ground-breaking structure which allowed for large expanses of glass on the front elevation.

Arguably the first assuredly modern building in Britain was New Ways in Northampton (1925). The house was commissioned by the industrial modeller W.J. Bassett-Lowke and designed by Peter Behrens. That a foremost Continental designer worked in the heart of steadfastly traditional England is not entirely surprising when Bassett-Lowke's previous house is considered; it was remodelled at Derngate by Charles Rennie Mackintosh, who had met Behrens through the Vienna Secession in the early 1900s. Indeed, the client transferred much of the interior detail from Derngate to New Ways, but it was with the exterior that Behrens sewed the first seeds of Modernism in England with the flat rendered brick surface, cantilevered door canopy and the arrangement of windows. Intersecting the front elevation is a vertical, V-profile-glazed projection accenting the central staircase from the first to the second storey, surmounted with black concrete fins which run along the whole roof.

The Scottish architect Thomas Smith Tait developed his modern architectural style with Le Chateau in 1927, built as part of a series of houses for workers and managers of the Crittall window company at Silver End in Essex. Here the proportions were played with to give a more Continental design, with white rendered brickwork and horizontal metal windows – fabricated, of course, by Crittall. The appearance of the house fell into the pattern of foreign examples and would not have seemed out of place at the Weissenhoff Siedlung. Also part of the Silver End development was a terrace of smaller houses showing a clear influence from Behrens's New Ways with V-shaped window projections. Tait, as part of Sir John Burnet Partners, had seen first-hand the exciting developments in France and The Netherlands and injected this new vocabulary into the Crittall buildings, which Henry Russell Hitchcock regarded as comparing favourably with the best examples of Modernism on the Continent.

But Silver End was just a tentative step towards a Modern Movement which was really only surface deep. One of Tait's partners in the project, Frederick McManus, confessed his reservations in a letter to the architectural historian Jeremy Gould in 1972, 'I worked enthusiastically on these houses but subsequently realized they were really the traditional house styled in the manner of the new architecture that was just beginning to emerge on the continent...'.

With the Daily Mail Ideal Home exhibition of 1928 this new direction in architecture was given a wider exposure. Elements of the style – the horizontal window, the white rendering – became popularized along with the emergence of Art Deco from the Paris Exposition des Artes Décoratif et Industriele of 1925 and became more widely used in housing schemes, particularly those on the south coast where more progressively and genuinely Modernist houses were later to appear.

The year 1927 saw the publication of one of the most important modern architectural texts in Britain. Frederick Etchell's translation of Le Corbusier's Vers Une Architecture. It was a key point in the formation of a British Modern Movement, the book itself presenting such a tantalizing example to progressive young architects, poised to emulate the new forms of the machine age, the '...masterly, correct and magnificent play of masses brought together in light.' Etchells himself took a role in these formative years, turning from Vorticist painting to architecture with his Crawfords building of 1929. Here he adopted the form of Le Corbusier with the ribbon windows and crisp rectilinear forms, and even nodded towards Mies van der Rohe's Barcelona exhibition pavilion of the same year with its chromed window mullions. It was the first modern office building in England and set the pace for later high-rise work with its exciting machine purity and art deco style.

In the same year as Behrens's New Ways, the Paris Exposition of 1925 was to have further influence on British architects with its rejection of historicism and emphasis on the moderne. With abundant examples of what became known as 'art deco', a contraction of the exhibition's full title, and tasters of Purism and Constructivism to influence young architects greatly, the Exposition was to have far-reaching effects on the British scene. The most significant building was Le Corbusier's Pavilion de l'Esprit Nouveau, a culmination of his work on what he called 'Immeubles' housing, a single habitation unit designed for an infinitely expandable apartment block. It involved simple, industrially produced components, the staircase, window frames and glass all of factory standard, the doors fabricated by the Ronier sheet metal company. The design took account of the use of space, light and air, all controlled within a reinforced concrete frame. The interior was a confluence of crafts and industry comprising Accasier modular storage units, bentwood Thonay chairs, Oriental rugs and South American pottery – a synthesis of hand and machine.

Le Corbusier's pavilion was to influence architects considerably who would later shape the British modern scene. It presented an entirely new attitude to aesthetic form and interior volume which was to be adopted by British modernists throughout the inter-war period. One architect in particular, the New Zealander Amyas Connell, found English attempts at modern architecture insipid and directionless when compared with the work of Le Corbusier. When he won a scholarship to the British School in Rome, Connell was to test his own ability with his first commission, a house for the School's director, Professor Ashmole. High and Over was built in 1929 at Amersham and marks ground zero for British Modernism. The influence from France is clear with its rigid plan, off-set by the 120-degree angle of the wings, the third-floor balcony a clear reference to Le Corbusier's Villa Stein of 1927, and the cantilevered roof canopy from Andre Lurçat's Villa Gugenbrühl, also of 1927. The interior has a spatial variety and excitement with its large, hexagonal central hall. With his references to beaux-arts planning and modern structure as well as the use of light, shade and surface from his interest in the baroque, Connell started a phase of architecture in England with something new and vital. The first rumblings had led to a serious attempt to emulate Continental theory.

New Blood

If there was a lack of direction in British modern architecture as Connell perceived it, then the influx of creative power from abroad served to inject the country with a fresh impetus and a new range of possibilities. Architects who are now considered the fathers of Modernism – Erich Mendelsohn, Walter Gropius and Marcel Breuer – came primarily to escape persecution in their native Germany, but also, perhaps inevitably, play a role in guiding British architecture in a new direction. Indeed, many of the architects who were involved in experimenting and supporting the modern style in Britain were from foreign climes – Amyas Connell and Basil Ward from New Zealand, Berthold Lubetkin and Serge Chermayeff from Russia and Raymond McGrath from Australia.

The first of the émigrés was Lubetkin, who travelled from Paris in 1930 and joined a group of rebellious Architectural Association students to form Tecton. Originally from the Caucasus, in the south-western Soviet Union, Lubetkin studied in Moscow and then Paris. He enrolled at the Atelier Perret where he learnt from Le Corbusier the techniques of building in concrete and quickly digested the 'five points' of architecture. In 1931 Tecton received its first commission, a building for two Congolese gorillas at Regent's Park Zoo, which was quickly followed by another to design the penguin pool, the latter becoming a famous landmark with its oval form and twin intertwining ramps.

The inexorable rise of Adolf Hitler and the Nazi Party fostered a new German ethic of Nationalism in the early 1930s. In terms of architecture this meant a return to the Neo-classical tradition of Karl Schinkel (1781–1841) and the Bavarian vernacular. The political significance of classical art and design in Nazi Germany was not so much a result of Hitler's interest in the subject but more from the nature of Modernism in the Weimar republic. The associations between the avant-garde and Communism, the only credible political threat to Hitler, meant that anything faintly left-wing had to be purged from the Fatherland and discredited as degenerate.

In the summer of 1933 Erich Mendelsohn, a Modernist and a Jew, moved from Germany to England with the intention of setting up a practice. He partnered Serge Chermayeff, with whom he was already acquainted, in an office on London's Oxford Street. It is clear from their first commission, a private house in Buckinghamshire called Shrubbs Wood, that Mendelsohn had lost nothing of his architectural verve and expressive visual qualities. The volumes are highly articulated, staggered and proportioned in a characteristic, low vertical form, reflecting earlier work in Germany. Clearly, Mendelsohn was intent on starting afresh in England, free from the constraints and persecution of Nazi Germany and continuing to push forward the possibilities in architectural form. Together Mendelsohn and Chermayeff produced some of Britain's iconic structures, including the De La Warr Pavilion at Bexhill (1935) and the Cohen house in Chelsea, London (1936).

In 1934 Walter Gropius arrived and formed a partnership with the British architect E. Maxwell Fry. Their first building together was also a private house, at 66 Old Church Street in Chelsea, for the playwright Benn Levy in 1935–36, sited on the adjacent plot to Mendelsohn and Chermayeff's Cohen house of the same year. Gropius and Fry's house presents an ambiguous face to the street, with intriguing curves enticing the eye towards the invisible, private spaces behind. The garage entrance is positioned next to the front door, voicing the ideology of machine and human coexistence and again refers back to Le Corbusier's Villa Stein. It also says much about the significance of the automobile to the moneyed classes of the 1920s and 1930s.

One of the last of the German émigrés to arrive in England was Marcel Breuer in 1935 and,

although primarily a designer of furniture in tubular steel at the Bauhaus, he had turned to architecture while still in Germany. In Britain he partnered Francis Yorke and they of all the émigré partnerships, embraced the use of reinforced concrete wholeheartedly.

The influx of foreign architects did much to breathe life into the 1930s scene in Britain. All but a few of the émigrés joined British architects and must have found these partnerships invaluable when encountering the convolutions of building practice in this country. In return, the native architects were able to work alongside the pioneers of Modernism and learn from their experience. Importantly, these strong associations indicated a desire for cohesion in the movement and almost

In Britain during the inter-war period the International Style invaded the leafy suburbs of Hampstead with, among other structures, Wells Coates' Isokon Lawn Road Flats,1934.

Ernö Goldfinger's own house at 1–3 Willow Road in Hampstead, London, 1939, was one of his first contributions to the Modern Movement in Britain; controversial in its day, the building was a comparatively unassuming presage of the architect's post-war buildings that would exert a much more forceful presence on the landscape.

use of reinforced concrete, and the seminal text on English vernacular architecture by Hermann Muthesius, Das Englische Haus, of 1904. In 1933 he moved to London with his new British wife Ursula Blackwell and occupied a flat in Highpoint 1, an important Modernist block in Hampstead by Lubetkin.

In 1939 Goldfinger built a small terrace of three houses close to Highpoint at 1–3 Willow Road, occupying number 2 for nearly forty years. This small-scale, brick-built structure was, in spite of the traditional materials, decidedly modern, but it does not even hint at the scale of his later high-rise work in London, explored in more detail in chapter 6.

Although serious about their work and their motivation to improve Britain's built environment, the Modernist architects lacked the cohesive spirit that had existed on the Continent. Efforts were made to bring the activities of these architects in Britain together in a collective unit and this came to fruition when the co-founder of the CIAM, Sigfried Giedion, approached the British architect Philip Morton Shand with the idea of forming a counterpart group here. Shand in turn contacted his fellow Briton Wells Coates and together they founded the Modern Architectural Research Society, otherwise known as MARS.

Their aims initially were to identify the problems of modern architecture and to move towards their solution. Their solidarity as a group was attributable as much, if not more, to their facing hostility or indifference from British society in general than to their unanimity in design philosophy. In fact, there were conflicts of viewpoint within the group and this served to erode the very unity that MARS desperately needed to survive. But in spite of divisions within the group, it continued to soldier on until 1957 when it was finally disbanded.

The real death knell to the International Modern style of architecture was the outbreak of war in 1939. This cataclysmic event and the subsequent years of conflict served to further fragment the movement and focus the world's attention away from new building styles. The architects of the Modern Movement continued to work with varying degrees of success. Walter Gropius, Marcel

certainly stemmed from the naturally collective nature of Modernism on the Continent. It was the strength of these associations that would prove vital to the survival of Modernism in Britain in the face of robust opposition.

One émigré architect of the 1930s was to have a greater influence on post-war architecture in Britain than any of the others. The Hungarian Ernö Goldfinger (1904–87) had studied in Paris at the École des Beaux Artes and with the atelier of August Perret, where he came into contact with Le Corbusier and Berthold Lubetkin. Goldfinger's key early influences were Perret and Corbusier's

The post-war period in North America was dominated by the glass and steel aesthetic espoused by Ludwig Mies Van der Rohe, seen here in the seminal Lake Shore Drive Apartments, Chicago, of 1950.

Breuer and Mies van der Rohe all emigrated to North America. Le Corbusier remained in France, although he worked on buildings throughout the world, including the United States and India. The native British Modernists were to be replaced by a younger, more radical element which were to set about reforming the CIAM in the post-war period.

By the late 1940s the notion of a common vocabulary in Modernist architecture, an International Style as had existed pre-war, began to fragment. This was due in part to growing generational differences in the Modern Movement, but also to the changing supply of raw materials, which, to an extent, dictated form and style. Le Corbusier turned to rough-cast concrete, or *béton brut*, as exemplified in the *Unité d'Habitation*, Marseille, 1952. Ludwig Mies van der Rohe developed the distinctive skeletal steel and glass aesthetic, rooted in his Barcelona pavilion of 1929. This lent itself perfectly to the skyscraping commissions he won in his adopted home of the United States, here seen at its best in the Lake Shore Drive Apartments, Chicago, of 1951. Although they were distinctively different approaches to the needs of modern architecture, as well as differing aesthetically, both 'styles' held much of interest and inspiration for the new generation of architects.

The Emergence of Brutalism

In the post-war years Le Corbusier had turned to a heavier, more monumental style of architecture, continuing to use the basic elements developed in the 1920s but adapting them to his new commissions. Concrete was no longer rendered or painted, it was largely left rough and unadorned in the form known as '*béton brut*'. One of the first of these where we see the seeds of Brutalism being sown is the Jaoul houses in Neuilly-sur-Seine, mentioned above, where brick and wood are mixed with concrete to form heavy, grounded volumes. Seen in context alongside his Duval factory at

Saint-Die (1946–50) and the *Unité d'Habitation* in Marseille (1947–53), what emerged from the offices of Le Corbusier was to have repercussions throughout the modern architectural world.

Britain emerged from the Second World War triumphant but severely damaged by the conflict. The Treasury was depleted and its urban landscape decimated by the blitz. Initially architecture in Britain was finding its feet and the divisions within the Modern Movement which emerged in the inter-war period continued to exist after 1945. There was a desire, particularly in the London County Council's Architects' Department, for building on a human scale, following Scandinavian examples and picturesque planning. The new breed of architects were keen to sweep these ideas aside in favour of something that genuinely met, as they saw it, the realities of modern life.

The second generation of modern architects began to drive the direction of the debate and set themselves apart from their elders in the CIAM. A splinter group, Team 10 (aka Team X), emerged in 1953, including Alison and Peter Smithson, for whom the group was of paramount importance. In the same year the Smithsons published designs for a house at Colville Place in Soho, London, using the term 'New Brutalism' for perhaps the first time in the accompanying text. As well as describing the nature of the materials, which were intended to be unfinished and unadorned wherever possible, the term was something of an in-joke. But the design theorist Reyner Banham seized upon it as emblematic of the new direction and the label was adopted by the rising stars of British modern architecture.

What emerged from the debate between 'ethic and aesthetic', as Banham described it, were some remarkable structures from both sides of the argument. Brutalism, though, was a very British phenomenon and may not have happened in quite the same way without the drive of eager, hungry young architects in this country willing to take on the elder statesmen of the CIAM, the New Humanists of the council architects' departments and the prevailing conservative taste of the general public. Brutalism spread from Britain to other countries, taking on distinctive characteristics in

Japan, France, Eastern Europe and the United States. One may also detect a wider cultural movement, of which Brutalist architecture was a part. In the fine arts, media, design and politics, Brutalism was an almost inevitable evolution of the Modern Movement.

The New Brutalism: Ethic or Aesthetic

In 1955, architectural historian Reyner Banham wrote a piece for *Architectural Review* in which he attempted to define the term 'New Brutalism'. More was yet to be said on the origins of the phrase, but Banham believed it had been coined by Alison and Peter Smithson in a way that seemed to work as a counterpoint to the term 'New Humanism'. What he was able to draw on were two key buildings, one complete and the other a concept. The built example was the Smithson's school at Hunstanton, completed in 1947, which by virtue of its logical plan, its use of unadorned materials and its clearly exposed structure made it the first truly Brutalist building in England. The concept project was a house in Soho, London, the plans for which were published in *Architectural Review* in 1953. In their write-up, the Smithsons used the term 'New Brutalism' for perhaps the first time in print. At this point, Brutalism was an emerging 'movement', and both the ethics and aesthetics implicit in the term were not yet fully formed. But it was, nevertheless, a *force majeure* worth exploring, which Banham did in much more detail just over ten years later, in 1966, when he published his book *The New Brutalism: Ethic or Aesthetic*. In this detailed biography of an architectural style, Banham traces its genesis as a concept, the development of an ethic and its evolution into an aesthetic.

As Banham perceived it, the immediate post-war period saw a reflection of the generational tensions that were being felt in the CIAM at the time. In Britain, though, the architectural scene

Book cover of Reyner Banham's The New Brutalism: Ethic or Aesthetic, *1966.*

(which seemed to centre, according to Banham, on the London County Council's Architects' Department) was beset with a struggle between Socialist Realism and something new that had yet to be solidified. This hardening of Communist idealism within the department was, perhaps, a natural symptom of the post-war Labour government and welfare state ethos. It looked back to William Morris and his Red House as an exemplar, as well as casting around for inspiration from other more mature welfare state architecture in countries like Sweden. In formal terms this meant brick structure, pitched roofs and picturesque planning, which was given the title 'New Humanism', something Banham saw as a reinvention of the Swedish term 'New Empiricism'. Against this backdrop we find the somewhat jocular use of 'Neo-Brutalist' by Hans Asplund in 1950. That term migrated to England, converging with the desire for a new architecture that responded to the realities of the day, and resolved into what became 'New Brutalism'.

In his book, Banham goes on to plot out the evolution of Brutalism, focusing initially on the work of Alison and Peter Smithson, to which he refers throughout. The theory of New Brutalism made real in the Smithsons' high school building at Hunstanton, embodying three key characteristics or 'truths' – truth to materials, truth to function and truth to topography– is written into the DNA of the movement. It is what drove the work, both theoretical and built, of the Smithsons, as well as that of others close to them in the profession and the wider arts, and their students and protégés.

The author also identifies an aesthetic of Brutalism and suggests that the genesis of this can be found in Le Corbusier's Maisons Jaoul (1956) at Neuilly-sur-Seine, to the west of Paris. The combination of brick and rough concrete, the arrangement of volumes, and the use of shape and surface texture were repeated or referenced in British architecture, most notably in Stirling and Gowan's flats at Ham Common (1958). The role of the ethic, from this point, becomes subsumed or even lost altogether as the aesthetic seems to take hold of the profession. Banham found, casting around the world, that the Brutalist style had been adopted in Japan, Italy, Spain, Chile and Switzerland. There are coincidences in style and apparent references that developed independently, suggesting to the author that the Brutalist style was almost inevitable, even without a handy label.

In spite of its spread around the world, Brutalism, Banham concludes, originated in Britain. The impact of British ideas on architectural theory and aesthetics in the immediate post-war years was undeniable and acknowledged by the likes of Renatio Pedio and Philip Johnson. But writing in 1966, Reyner Banham believed that New Brutalism was essentially over. Modern architecture had reached a level of maturity that transcended the label. He conceded, though, that the style might well continue as a 'going concern' and even throw up a few surprises.

Chapter 2

Civic Building

As Britain began the slow and painful process of regeneration after the Second World War, one of the key goals of the government and local authorities was a comprehensive building programme. This did not begin and end with housing, although that was by far the top priority. Both the Labour and the Conservative Party made clear in their manifestos for elections during the 1950s and the 1960s that the tools of local government needed to be strong, capable and up to date. The Conservative winning manifesto of 1955 had this to say about local authorities: 'The social policy we have outlined will make heavy demands on the energies and capacity of local authorities up and down the country. They must be strong and well-equipped if they are to carry out these responsibilities effectively.'

The immediate post-war period saw Modernism continue International Style traditions as well as Scandinavian influences seen in one of the first major structures of the period, the Royal Festival Hall on London's South Bank by Leslie Martin and others, 1951.

Civic building, therefore, was very much part of the grand plan and the latest materials and building techniques were employed to solve the problems the nation faced. A happy by-product of this process would be, it must have been hoped, a strengthening of civic pride and community spirit. Many new structures, particularly town halls and civic offices, were tendered by open competition and it seems that the work of progressive young architects was often favoured.

The Festival of Britain and the Royal Festival Hall

Although the Exchequer's coffers were worryingly empty, an initiative was launched to reinvigorate and thrill a society beginning to emerge from the yoke of wartime privation. It would be a showcase for British design, technology, science, the arts and industrial prowess. It would be a sorely needed tonic for all to enjoy. It was the Festival of Britain and an unassuming plot of land on London's South Bank was cleared and prepared, filled with exhibits and opened to the public on 3 May 1951. The two key structures of the Festival were the Dome of Discovery and the Royal Festival Hall. The latter was designed by the London County Council and a principal team of three: Leslie Martin, Robert Matthew and Peter Moro.

The site itself was far from ideal as the starting point for a structure of this size and complexity. To begin with, the ground water level was some 3.7m (12ft) higher than the foundations needed to be laid and so the whole site had to be excavated and drained into specially dug wells. In order just to do that the site had first to be cleared of the foundations of earlier structures.

Although the internal frame and roof were of reinforced concrete tied together with steel

trusses, it was considered not appropriately decorative to be left unadorned and so a veneer cladding of Portland stone and Hadene marble was used. The interior spaces were lavished with all manner of finishes, including elm-laminate panelling and perforated plastic sheeting. The roof was covered with copper and the window frames were of lacquered aluminium with steel mullions, where structural support was needed.

The acoustics were obviously a key factor in the build and so some of the materials, such as the elm cladding in the auditorium and the use of large, plate-glass sections in the windows, were chosen specifically to aid these. Indeed, the design of the hall took inspiration from many venerable concert venues around Europe, such as the Gewandhaus in Leipzig of Martin Gropius (great uncle of Walter Gropius) and Heino Schmieden, of 1884.

On the river front of the Royal Festival Hall one can see the influence from Lubetkin's Highpoint II in the arrangement of contained and recessed windows and volumes.

The rear elevation of the Festival Hall (refaced) seen from the Hayward Gallery plaza presents a much heavier and more robust facade with the massing of volumes presaging later Brutalist structures.

Accommodating 3,500, the Royal Festival Hall was the biggest concert venue in Britain at the time of its opening. The overall structure was Palladian in proportions, with its curved raised roof and symmetrical front elevation. Stylistically the building leaned emphatically towards the International Style, but elements that would later feature prominently in British Modernism – the heavier, more grounded form, the unadorned concrete – are important to note. Yet the old order predominated in the design, but this should come as no surprise when one considers that the original concept was developed barely two years after VE Day, when the unfinished business of the pre-war British Modern Movement still lingered in the industry. The fact that Moro was a former associate of Lubetkin gives perspective to the marked similarities with Highpoint II.

The interior was painstakingly detailed, with a large and spacious foyer which was intended to allow a wide range of people to come and go and interact. The central auditorium was built to float above a basement level 'box' in which were housed restaurants and bars, this lower space then also acting as an insulator against the noise travelling up from the underground railway.

This was the first important public building after the war and the architects approached it with enthusiasm, taking great care over the details and the materials, especially the latter, which were sourced direct from the docks, where the most recent shipments could be reserved. In more recent years the building has been tampered with, but, in spite of that, it became the first post-war building to achieve Grade 1 listing. More recently a comprehensive refurbishment has gradually returned both the interior and the exterior to something of their original clarity and integrity.

While the New Brutalists, as they would come to be known, regarded this Scandinavian-flavoured reference to the International Style as representing everything they despised in modern building, Leslie Martin's place in the story of Brutalism is important nonetheless. His position on the LCC allowed him to promote the work of younger architects, including Alison and Peter Smithson. And later, Martin would fix his place in the Brutalist canon, working with Colin St John Wilson to design Harvey Court hostel at Gonville and Caius College, Cambridge, in 1962.

TUC Headquarters

There were few really meaty public projects for modern architects to get their hands on during the late 1940s and early 1950s, but those that did come along were handled with care and optimism. The lingering influence of the first generation Modernists can be easily found in such projects. A typical example of this was Congress House on Great Russell Street, London, another important structure of its day, completed in 1957.

David Du R. Aberdeen, Congress House, London, 1957, Dyott Street elevation. Its curvaceous lines recalling Brinkman & Van der Vlugt's Van Nelle factory at Rotterdam, the ribbon windows and smooth stone cladding almost pure International Style.

David Du R. Aberdeen, Congress House, 1957, front elevation with sculpture by Bernard Meadows in bronze emblematic of trade unionism, the main volume behind floating above the pavement on slender pilotis.

The concept of a new headquarters for the Trades Union Congress germinated in 1944, but it was not until 1948 that a competition was launched to find the best design. Of the 181 entries it was the work of David Du R. Aberdeen which won. The main strength of his design lay in placing the 500-seat conference hall below ground level, leaving the upper floors free to be fed light from a central courtyard. The exterior borrowed much from pre-war Modernism, primarily Le Corbusier's. The main structure floats above a recessed ground floor, raised on pilotis, and ribbon windows run the length of the exposed elevations. Aberdeen also nods towards Lubetkin

with the recessed upper floor on the front facade, again mirroring Highpoint II, as did the Festival Hall, and also with the vertical row of five seemingly frivolous balconies on the Dyott Street elevation. Also on this side is a playfully curved glass section which, although not as pronounced, brings to mind the Van Nelle factory near Rotterdam of 1929, designed by Johannes Brinkmann and associates.

Inside the courtyard a sculpture by Jacob Epstein was commissioned and completed in 1955. This war memorial takes the form of a stylized pietà, carved where it stands from a single block of stone imported from Italy and

David Du R. Aberdeen, Congress House, 1957. The interior courtyard shows influences from Expressionism and Constructivisim, particularly in the marble sculpture of the Pieta by Jacob Epstein which contains strong echoes of massive Soviet public art.

weighing 10 tons. Outside the Great Russell Street entrance stands another piece of public art, a large bronze sculpture by Bernard Meadows of the spirit of trade unionism. Here Meadows is in a much less stylistic mode than his other work of the same period, with two figures, a stronger standing man helping a weaker recumbent figure. The TUC in its concept for Congress House saw it as an opportunity to embrace not just new architecture but the arts as well and the two are clearly married here in Bloomsbury. Of course, architecture has always been closely allied with the arts, sculpture in particular, and Brutalism was no exception. Meadows himself was one of five new artists who exhibited to much acclaim at the

Venice Biennale of 1952, another of whom was Eduardo Paolozzi, who formed a close friendship with Alison and Peter Smithson.

Where the Royal Festival Hall and Congress House drew some of their inspiration from the likes of Le Corbusier, the divergence between these two buildings and the work of the French Modernist in the post-war years is quite pronounced. By 1947 work had begun on Le Corbusier's Unité d'Habitation in Marseille, a monumental slab structure in rough-cast concrete, heralding the full blossoming of Brutalism on the Continent. By contrast, these two British buildings were restrained although refined, using polished stone rather than concrete as the primary facing material. For the time being, public buildings utilized a form of

David Du R. Aberdeen, Congress House, 1957, Dyott Street facade with seemingly frivolous balconies highly reminiscent of Lubetkin's Highpoint I.

Berthold Lubetkin and Tecton, Highpoint I, London, 1935. The curving balconies, though more practical than those at Congress House, nevertheless provided the same texture to the exterior.

C B Pearson Son & Partners, Carlisle Civic Centre, 1965. A building seeming undecided whether to embrace the emerging Brutalist aesthetic or the established Miesian form.

C B Pearson Son & Partners, Carlisle Civic Centre, 1965. The massing of volumes and predominance of concrete are very much of the period, though with less elegance than the pure glass and steel 'tower and podium' structures like Castrol House or Euston Tower.

Modernism that had not yet matured into something more arresting, but importantly the new style was experiencing wider acceptance and working its way into the mainstream.

Outside London

During the 1960s we begin to see the influence of the new Brutalists in other areas of architectural design – housing, commercial, educational, for example – feeding back into civic building. Carlisle's new town hall and civic centre by

Charles B. Pearson Son and Partners, completed in 1965, took the Miesian 'tower and podium', format but with a reinforced concrete skeletal frame that clearly drew inspiration from the growing Brutalist trend. Indeed, the lower octagonal tower is strikingly similar to the Smithsons' *Economist* building completed in the same year.

By 1968 when Shire Hall, Robert Harvey's civic offices in Flintshire, was built, the Massive phase of Brutalism was in full swing. Known locally as 'Legoland', this complex comprises a long, seven-storey, slab block with a three-storey quadrangle behind. The distinctive exterior elevations have concrete 'frames' facing alternating windows, giving the building a somewhat ambiguous appearance from a distance, but one of sober solidity befitting a local authority headquarters. The arrangement of the windows and the scale of the blocks are highly reminiscent of Eero Saarinen's United States Embassy building at Grosvenor Square, London (1960).

Although Huddersfield's Queensgate Market is essentially a commercial structure, it formed part of a civic plan conceived by the Corporation which began before the outbreak of war and culminated in this structure which was completed in 1970. Here we see the Massive phase of Brutalism in all its glory, with a striking collection of asymmetrical roof canopy projections enclosed within a stone-clad perimeter wall, topped with undulating fenestrations and adorned with a series of terracotta panel sculptures by Fritz Steller.

The Corporation employed the property developer Murrayfield Real Estate to manage the project, which, in turn, brought in the J. Seymour Harris Partnership as architects. The concept for the market was developed by Gwyn Roberts, and formed part of a larger, four-part scheme for the city centre. It was a traditional space enclosed with inverted, tent-like overlapping canopies set at different heights to let light through and give the impression of an open-air market, while affording protection from the elements. The whole roof structure comprises twenty-one square-section columns between 3.5 and 7.5m

(11.5 and 24.8ft) high, each surmounted with a hyperbolic paraboloid canopy cantilevered off-centre. Between the canopies at the outside edges, an innovative glazing system was constructed which was designed to adjust with the natural movement of the roof structure. This arrangement of umbrella canopies on heavy columns bears a resemblance to Le Corbusier's Palace of Labour pavilion for the 1961 Turin Exhibition.

From the outside, the market hall presents a striking profile set between the elevated ring road on one side and up a steeply sloping site to the town hall on the other. Immediately arresting are Steller's series of terracotta panels which project like square carbuncles, carved in high relief with sinuous forms. Here again we see the amalgamation of architecture and fine art with a highly successful partnership. The impact of Queensgate market would be so much less without the panels; they provide depth, incident and cultural context. All too often public art exists for itself and its purpose is often lost on the observer. Here in Huddersfield, though, the art has a definite function.

ABOVE RIGHT: C B Pearson Son & Partners, Carlisle Civic Centre, 1965, detail of lower block showing a strong similarity with the Smithsons' Economist Building.

RIGHT: J Seymour Harris Partnership (Gwyn Roberts), Queensgate Market, Huddersfield, 1970. Standing like a walled city with its undulating roof canopies but still inviting one to take a more lingering glance to study the terracotta panels of Fritz Steller.

Preston Bus Station

The post-war regeneration of towns and cities was partly motivated by the rebuilding work that took place following significant bomb damage, but it also gained momentum as an opportunity to look forward to accommodating increased vehicle traffic, improving communications between con-urbations and developing consumer trade. The Preston area, by-passed by what would become the M6 motorway, was in danger of becoming economically depressed, and so in the late 1950s it became part of a new town expansion plan that was envisaged to grow and develop between the 1960s and 1980s. Part of that plan was to link Preston to the M6 and a new motorway, the M61, which would create easier access to Greater Manchester. To improve communications within the town, a new bus terminal and car park were proposed in 1959. The Preston Corporation chose Building Design Partnership (BDP), then known as Grenfell Baines and Hargreaves, to carry out the design.

The original concept went through a number of changes before the design for a bus station with a multi-storey car park above was settled on by 1965. This scheme would accommodate eighty buses and parking for 1,100 vehicles, and incorporate a passenger concourse and offices. BDP came back with an estimated overall cost of £1,062,000 (equivalent to around £20 million today). The whole site had a footprint of 96 × 188m (314 × 616ft), inside which was the concourse, including waiting room, small shops and offices, and the bus company canteen, altogether occupying 30 × 171m (100 × 560ft).

Arup Associates were engaged as the project engineers, and they specified a ribbed pre-cast concrete floor-panel construction, the ribs articulated in the curved balustrades of the car park,

Grenfell Baines and Hargreaves (later BDP), Preston Bus Station, 1969. Front elevation, showing the iconic concrete fins of the carpark storeys.

Grenfell Baines and Hargreaves (later BDP), Preston Bus Station, 1969.
Terminus interior with passenger waiting areas.

which gives the building its distinctive profile. Passengers enter the concourse via three subways, and the use of external landscaping, boulders and shoulder-height concrete barriers segregates foot traffic from cars and buses. The double-height concourse itself is fully glazed along the side elevations, with sliding doors giving access to each bus terminal. Cars enter and exit the car park via ramps at the north and south ends, and there are eight internal ramps connecting the floors.

Arup insisted on an excellent finish throughout and imposed exacting standards on the construction contractors. Exposed concrete, much of it cast on site in fibreglass moulds, had to be of uniform colour throughout, which demanded fine-tuning the casting process to achieve the desired quality. Visible structural columns were sand-blasted to expose the aggregate within the concrete mix. The end result, completed in 1969, is a superb and lasting testament to Arup's attention to detail.

Added to this were the architects' own design flourishes, including custom-fitted, oiled iroko-wood seats, doors, handrails and barrier rails.

Bespoke clocks and signage also give the internal space the scale and romance of an airport terminal, as if the station were a gateway to international travel destinations.

As in Cumbernauld, Preston's expected population boom never materialised, and so the city was graced with a bus station rather too large for the traffic it ultimately accommodated. But its grandeur endeared it to the local population, who recently saved it from demolition after much hard campaigning; it now has Grade II listed status and is protected as a significant post-war structure.

In the Massive phase of Brutalism the use of concrete becomes more prevalent and inventive, most often in its rough-cast state as advocated by Le Corbusier but moulded into exciting forms that immediately grasp the attention. The practice of Gollins, Melvin & Ward was a key player in the post-war period, perhaps because they could adapt quite radically to the needs of the brief and the style demanded by the client. And so within their portfolio can be found Mies-style glass slab type buildings, such as Castrol House on the Marylebone Road, London (1959), as well as heavy Brutalist structures such as their Woking Centre Halls and library completed in 1975. In this last complex the use of concrete and brick together created a distinctive, solid and yet elegant presence.

Grenfell Baines and Hargreaves (later BDP), Preston Bus Station, 1969.
Arup Associates' distinctive ribbed, pre-cast concrete balustrades.

J Seymour Harris Partnership (Gwyn Roberts), Queensgate Market, Huddersfield, 1970. Steller's panels take inspiration from South American art and provide needed texture to the exterior, unifying the elements of concrete and stone cladding.

The two elements of the complex, the Centre Halls and the library, were designed together and sited close to the new town square and shopping precinct, on the basis that the majority of visitors would be on foot but with allowance for cars to gain close access as well. The structures essentially comprised a series of canted oblong forms, with load-bearing brick mainly at ground-floor level supporting pre-cast concrete first-floor levels. Stair towers, one of which acted as a link between the two main structures, were faced entirely in brick. But the concrete first-floor volumes with canted roof lines formed the most distinctive profile by the use of floor-to-ceiling, vertical strip windows recessed into brise-soleil ribs.

Within the 2,675sq.m (3,200sq.yd) Centre Halls was accommodation for stage and screen performances, with raked seating for 250 people and a main hall for meetings or dinners, each served by ancillary foyers, bars, dressing rooms and retiring rooms. In addition, there were four further meeting rooms capable of seating up to forty, and a manager's office. The interior walls were faced with brick or beech veneer, the floors were either beech strip or carpet. The library maintained the same design theme, with brick-faced ground floor and pre-cast concrete first floor with identical strip windows. The main entrance facing the town square was slightly recessed, with the first floor projecting out and supported on square-section pilotis. On the ground floor, the main lending library could hold over 40,000 volumes with a further 6,000 in the reference library on the first floor. A central staircase provided access to the first floor and was set on one side of a wide, square gallery, creating a sense of light and openness to the interior and linking the two spaces visually. Administrative spaces on the ground floor, including loading dock, rest room, boiler room, reserve room and offices, were grouped together in their own single-storey unit on the south-west corner of the building. In addition to the reference library, the first floor also boasted an exhibition space and a lecture theatre with seating for a hundred.

The Centre Halls formed part of a larger plan for Woking town centre, which began with the Centre Pool, also designed by Gollins, Melvin & Ward and completed in 1973. Sited at the north-west corner of the scheme, the pool stood away from the Centre Halls and library beside the ring road and car parks. To overcome the problem of underground water resulting from close proximity to the Basingstoke canal, the pool itself was set above ground, the space underneath partly taken up by the plant room, working in much the same 'egg-on-a-box' principle as Leslie Martin's Royal Festival Hall. The main building was accessed via a broad Corbusian double ramp running the length of one side.

J Seymour Harris Partnership (Gwyn Roberts), Queensgate Market, Huddersfield, 1970. The interior roof 'umbrellas' are virtuoso concrete structures providing shelter and light within their sturdy embrace.

Inside, a double-height space housed the main pool and a smaller nursery pool, enclosed with tall, ribbon windows along two sides, glazed with one-way, dark-brown tinted glass. Behind the steeply raked seating on one side were the changing rooms and above the nursery pool an enclosed glass-fronted cafe overlooking the main pool.

In Woking we see a cohesive solution to the rebuilding and updating of civic amenities.

Although standing out starkly against the largely red-brick Victorian buildings of the town, the scale and layout of the plan managed to complement rather than dominate the older structures. But if Brutalism could work in the form of stand-alone structures amid much older ones, how would it perform when directly attached to one? The answer to this can be found in Belfast with the Ulster Museum extension of 1972 by Francis Pym and Partners.

Northern Ireland

The original Ulster Museum was founded by the City Council to house the combined collections of antiquities and fine art belonging to the Belfast Natural History Society and Belfast Corporation. Like many public buildings, the design was decided by open competition, won by James Cumming Wynnes and sited within the Botanic Gardens and

Park in Stranmillis. Construction was interrupted by the First World War and, by the time it opened in 1929, less than half the original plan had been built at a cost of £90,000. What resulted was a U-shaped, Neo-classical building in Portland stone with the 2,880sq.m (3,445sq.yd) of display space arranged on three floors. The rusticated walls with recessed bays supported by Ionic columns were typical of the grandiose tradition in museum building, following the likes of Smirke's British Museum and Wilkie's National Gallery in London. In 1961 the Museum became a national institution with its own board of trustees and funding from central government. Shortly after, a proposal was tabled by the trustees and the Ministry of Finance to extend Wynnes's original building and finally complete it.

Another open competition was launched to do this, judged by Leslie Martin, architect of the Royal Festival Hall, and the winning design this time was that of Francis Pym and Partners (and was to be their only major work). The project began unhappily for Northern Ireland as the disturbances began there before it was completed. Mirroring the turbulence of the country, Pym's relationship with the project and its patrons was also volatile, eventually causing him to leave part way through, an event likened to Jorn Utzon's departure from the Sydney Opera House. Pym would not return to see the work completed, going back only long after leaving the architectural profession to find the building had suffered some disappointing alterations.

Pym's vision was to extrapolate the rustication so that the old literally melts into the new, an undulating concrete block with interconnected volumes projecting randomly as if the whole structure had been frozen in the process of exploding outwards.

Francis Pym, Ulster Museum Extension, 1972. The heavy Brutalist concrete structure cleverly melds with the earlier neo-classical building by extending the rustication through from one to the other. The seemingly random projections give the extension a highly sculptural appearance. (Image courtesy of Aiden McMichael)

Exterior details owe much to the post-war work of Le Corbusier – the courtyard plan and the decorative balconies from La Tourette Monastery, Lyons, of 1960 and the curving entrance canopy from the parliament building at Chandigarh, Punjab, of 1956. The interior was designed with a spiral route around the galleries which has been likened to Frank Lloyd Wright's Guggenheim Museum, although in concept rather than appearance. Indeed, here the spiral served as a rather ingenious means of connecting the new dynamic spaces with Wynnes's original, three-floor building. Like the Congress Hall, it was built around a central courtyard, although enclosed, and this served as a further display space in the heart of the building.

In order to complete the project the original building had to undergo structural alterations and the whole space, old and new, to be united with common design features. While the new building had few windows, meaning that the galleries had to rely on artificial light, the old part was similarly converted to produce a consistent interior feel. The marriage of the spiral extension and three-storey original structure, while providing a neat solution to the problem, resulted in a considerable challenge for the trustees to design the displays and signage in such a way as to prevent visitors from becoming completely disorientated.

When Pym left the project in 1968 the work was completed by J.F. Harrison from the Ministry of Finance, but this did not present any significant changes to the design either inside or out. Although rubber floor tiles, lighting gantries, air conditioning and heating were installed, almost nothing else was. The walls and the ceilings were left unfinished and ready for dressing. This left all of the interior fittings to be completed by the Museum itself at a cost of over £300,000 by the time it opened on 30 October 1972. What resulted was a 5,400sq.m (6,460sq.yd), state-of-the-art national museum that Ulster could be proud of, although at a cost of nearly twice the £382,000 estimate.

The City of London

Another example of how a new and modern extension to an existing historic building could work can be found in the City of London at the Guildhall. The original building was one of the oldest in the City, a stone structure faced in ashlar and

dating to the early fifteenth century, which had been refaced in the Neo-Gothic style in the 1780s, extended to the east in the nineteenth century, with a library and suffered some bomb damage during the Second World War. Sir Giles Gilbert Scott was commissioned to redesign the damaged roof and then continued to work with his son Richard on extending the building, starting in 1955.

Giles and Richard Scott, City of London Guildhall west wing extension, 1974. The main structure seen across the courtyard showing its interaction with the 18th-century facade of the original Guildhall.

Giles and Richard Scott, City of London Guildhall west wing extension, 1974. The umbrella canopies took Gothic detail from the older Guildhall and re-interpreted it in pre-cast concrete.

Giles and Richard Scott, City of London Guildhall west wing extension, 1974. On the main west wing block more Gothic imagery was brought to bear, the structure raised on heavy shaped columns.

It was Richard who continued the work on the west wing extension after his father's death in 1960, construction being completed in 1974 to house the library and civic offices for the City of London. Extending from the west elevation of the original Guildhall was an L-shaped, four-storey block with glazed frontage within pre-cast vertical beams and extending forward from this on the south front was a single storey with curtain-glazed frontage behind an undulating canopy of angular concrete umbrellas supported by tapering beams, reflecting the Gothic detail of the medieval building connected to it. Projecting southward and enclosing the courtyard, the

block continues, faced with pre-cast facing slabs and vertical beams, again reflecting the Gothic style, and raised at first-floor level on tapering columns. Within the courtyard on the east elevation, a large Alderman's Court of lobed cuboid form was added, with undulating geometric base, raised on four large, tapering columns to match those of the main block.

The concrete was coloured pale cream to match the dominant eighteenth-century facade and on the facing panels mixed with coarse aggregate and polished. The result was criticized by some for failing to integrate with the older structures and by the early 1980s it was already

Birmingham

The Massive period of Brutalism coincided with tremendous growth in civic building and redevelopment. The cities that had suffered so much during the blitz now began to benefit from the influx of money under the United States Marshall Plan and the growth in industries retooled from serving the war effort to supplying Britain and the rest of the world with new and exciting products. The country's second city, Birmingham, was subject to a grand plan of redevelopment with commercial and civic architecture combined. At the heart of this was the centenary square with its striking central library by John H.D. Madin & Partners, completed in 1974. This structure, like few others in the country, was unashamedly modernist, highly fashionable but remained practical and eminently mindful of its function.

From the outside, the library is a forceful structure, pressing its terraced profile against the sky like an inverted pyramid or a giant stack of books. Without any prior knowledge of its purpose one would be hard put to guess at what goes on inside as it presents an ambiguous face to the world. But the stepped form tapering in at the base invites one forward and few would be able to overcome their curiosity from driving them to enter and explore within. The open-plan interior, like that of Woking library, makes for a flexible space for storage, work and study, while the unique structure provides an environment designed to protect the book stock from harmful UV radiation.

John Madin was a local architect, born in Moseley, and so had a regional perspective on his projects, giving them an integrity that might have been lacking had anyone else won the commissions. Seen as part of a city-wide scheme, the library, though arresting to look at, is a harmonious structure, working in partnership with the surrounding structures. Among Madin's other work in the city is the Chamber of Commerce building and the Mail and Post building. To look at these structures gives an impression of the breadth of skill in the Madin partnership,

Giles and Richard Scott, City of London Guildhall west wing extension, 1974. Though the proportions are classical, the massing and the tactile exterior are Brutalist.

considered dated. The passage of time has, though, had a posititve effect and the addition of Richard Scott's 1990s post-modern Art Gallery on the east side of the courtyard completed the picture and provided an interesting interplay of styles from medieval to contemporary through Modernist. The west wing was another example of attention to detail and care over the quality of materials, with a strong, long-term vision of its future. But it is also a solid Brutalist building, showing how the style could be adapted to integrate with much older structures by taking on stylized versions of their characteristics.

John H Madin and Partners, Birmingham Central Library, 1974. Originally intended to be faced in stone, the concrete here does well to live up to the brief and the library has become an iconic Brutalist structure with its 'inverted ziggurat' profile. (Image courtesy of Elliott Brown)

much like Gollins, Melvin & Ward, able to adapt to Corbusian chunky concrete forms as well as Miesian glass and steel slabs. Clearly throughout the Massive period both schools were to be found in British building and they seemed to happily coexist even within the walls of one architectural practice and the confines of a single city.

The 'slab and podium' format which resonates throughout the post-war period in the work of Mies van der Rohe and his followers found its way into many urban schemes in Britain. It was universally exemplified by Skidmore, Owings & Merrill's Lever House, New York, of 1952 which set the template for such British buildings as Gollins, Melvin & Ward's Castrol House and Andrew Renton's Thorn House, both in London and completed in 1959, as well as G.S. Hay and Gordon Tait's Co-operative Insurance Tower in Manchester (1962),

and the Mail and Post building by John Madin in Birmingham (1960). The arrangement of a low-rise podium supporting a slab tower was not, however, completely confined to the Miesian steel and glass school of architecture.

A sublime Brutalist version of the slab and podium may be found in Wrexham with the Police Headquarters building by the Clwyd County Architects' Department and Stuart Brown, completed in 1976 at a cost of £775,000. This striking building dominates the town, although it was purposely built under 42m (137ft) tall in order to prevent it from overshadowing the town's other prominent structure, St Giles Church. The podium part is essentially L-shaped with one section raised to first-storey level in order to accommodate the undulating site and create a drive-through section with access to the loading bays and car park. The podium part contained an amenity wing including a canteen and recreational facilities. In the centre of the L a narrow stilt supports the central, fourteen-storey office tower which projects outwards on slanting wing cantilevers. Approached from the west, there is a wide staircase set into one corner of the podium, the roof of which is formed by the projecting first storey, leading to the main public entrance. But from all other sides the building presents an enigmatic face, although well fenestrated, standing like a redoubtable fortress. While the ground-floor levels are faced in dark grey brick, the upper levels from the first floor are clad in ribbed and unadorned concrete, adding to the effect of an impenetrable castle, able to withstand riot or siege.

RIGHT: *Clwyd County Council (Stuart Brown), North Wales Police Headquarters, Wrexham, 1976. A Brutalist interpretation of the tower and podium arrangement.*

BELOW: *Clwyd County Council (Stuart Brown), North Wales Police Headquarters, Wrexham, 1976. The use of moulded concrete cladding provides a fortified feel to the structure which is almost forbidding, befitting its primary function.*

Clwyd County Council (Stuart Brown), North Wales Police Headquarters, Wrexham, 1976. The main tower is cantilevered on angled stanchions, raising it above the podium so that it floats over the undulating site.

Clwyd County Council (Stuart Brown), North Wales Police Headquarters, Wrexham, 1976. At the entrance front the austere concrete is mitigated by the use of larger steel framed glass sections which contrast with the slender 'arrow slit' windows of the tower.

Basil Spence

Another example of the Brutalist tower can be found at 50 Queen Anne's Gate, London, with Basil Spence's building for the Home Office. It is highly reminiscent of Ernesto Rogers and Enrico Peressutti's Torre Velasca in Milan, completed nearly twenty years before, the fenestrated tower with the top section of storeys projecting outwards on cantilevers, so that the whole appears mushroom-shaped. Torre Velasca itself was based on medieval fortresses, and when one looks at Torrechiara Castle in Parma, for example, one can see where the inspiration came from. Spence's approach to 50 Queen Anne's Gate, although on a smaller scale, must surely have been derived from a similar inspiration and the result with its canted corners and knopped base seems neater and more convincingly sturdy than Rogers and Peresutti's tower.

But 50 Queen Anne's Gate was forcefully Brutalist in the Massive tradition with its use of unadorned concrete and the unconventional arrangement of volumes. The 30,000sq.m (35,900sq.yd) of space were arranged on fourteen floors, the top two of which project outwards, decorated with ribbed brise-soleil around the narrow slit windows, accentuating the fortress element, as if those windows were actually designed for archers to shoot through.

As the 1970s drew to a close, the architectural landscape began to change. There were seemingly conflicting influences from all over the world, but instead of fragmenting and pulling the profession apart, this heterogeneous mixture of styles and period references began to grow into a style of its own. This was to become Post-Modernism. In Britain, like other northern European countries, domestic, commercial and civic architecture moved towards a more human scale and more traditional materials and forms which interpreted something deeply rooted in the public psyche. This recipe of familiar ingredients; pitched tile roofs, brick walls and casement windows, evolved into the predominant form for the nation, Neo-vernacular. But before this became fully realized, Modernism went through a transitional phase where forms and materials began to change and merge.

A classic example of Transitional Brutalism in civic building is Spence's Kensington Town Hall and Library, completed in 1976. The original design for the complex was conceived in

Basil Spence, 50 Queen Anne's Gate, London (now Ministry of Justice), 1976. A tour de force in concrete; brutal and yet a unified scheme of great quality.

Basil Spence, 50 Queen Anne's Gate, London (now Ministry of Justice), 1976. The main tower with its projecting top section inspired by Italian medieval castles.

SIR BASIL SPENCE (1907–76)

Spence was born in Bombay to Scottish parents, but from 1919 grew up in Edinburgh. He studied architecture at Edinburgh College of Art, gaining experience along the way by producing drawings for practising architects in the city. A significant break came in 1929 when he secured an internship for a year in the London offices of Sir Edwin Lutyens, whose work was later to greatly influence him. His studies continued in the evenings at the Bartlett School of Architecture before he returned to Edinburgh in 1930 to complete his studies at the ECA. Upon graduating, he established a practice with fellow ECA graduate William Kininmonth, working primarily on private residential projects and exhibition pavilions. While Spence's clients predominantly tended towards the Neo-classical in their taste, there were some opportunities for him to apply Modernist principles, namely at Southside Garage in Edinburgh in 1933 and at Gribloch House in Stirlingshire in 1939. In the latter, designed for John Colville of the Colville steel family, the attention to detail, the subtle and economic use of style, the clipped and precise geometry of his post-war work can be seen emerging.

After the Second World War, Spence was to take a key role in shaping Britain's built environment with structures that remain iconic today. Like Le Corbusier, Spence played with materials, mixing traditional and modern, and could shift from sublime geometry to clashing asymmetry, from the humanity of brick to the brutality of concrete. He continued to design exhibition buildings, including the 'Sea and Ships' pavilion at the Festival of Britain, 1951, and the British Pavilion at Expo '67 in Montreal. The latter was a classic example of the Massive period, with its sharp angular forms and inverted terraced structure in ribbed concrete, presaging Madin's Birmingham Central Library.

Although Spence's practice was based in London, he maintained strong links with Scotland, designing the Duncanrig High School in East Kilbride, 1953, a high-rise housing development at Hutchesontown, Glasgow, 1962, the library at Edinburgh University, 1967, and Glasgow Airport, 1966. He also produced work for overseas briefs, including the striking New Zealand Parliament Buildings in Wellington (1964), affectionately known as 'the Beehive', and a Brutalist tour de force in the form of the British Embassy in Rome, completed in 1971.

Civic building formed a considerable part of Spence's work and included large-scale, multi-use projects such as the Sunderland Civic Centre, completed in 1970, the vocabulary of which, with its terraced hexagonal arrangement and use of brick and concrete together, was to appear again perhaps more strikingly in his scheme for Kensington Town Hall and Library, described in this chapter.

the mid-1960s and was remarkably prescient. It was opened only ten months after the Wrexham Police Headquarters, but the two schemes contrast starkly, one with both feet firmly in the Massive period while the other is clearly Transitional.

The red-brick exterior complements the surrounding mainly Victorian houses as well as the neighbouring Neo-classical library by Vincent Harris which was completed in 1960. The use of concrete on the Civic centre's exterior was kept to a minimum, acting as much as adornment as structurally, and playfully mirroring the masonry window mullions and porches of the surrounding buildings. On the Hornton Street elevation, Spence created more interplay with the opposing structures by creating brise-soleil in brick which project in sympathy with the window bays opposite and the architect was careful to scale his project so that it complemented rather than dwarfed the neighbouring houses. Also on Hornton Street the first floor is cantilevered over the pavement to provide shelter, with much of the structure raised on ribbed, square-section, concrete columns, giving vehicular access to parking areas within. The ceilings here are inset with lighting to prevent these inner spaces from suffering too much gloom and this also creates an inviting and positive atmosphere, drawing the eye in to investigate the intriguing interplay of spaces and geometric volumes with little glimpses of Campden Hill Road on the other side.

RIGHT: *Basil Spence, 50 Queen Anne's Gate, London (now Ministry of Justice), 1976. The visceral quality of the massing with the huge 'fish tank' window projections at first-floor level is a Brutalist masterclass.*

BELOW: *Basil Spence, Kensington and Chelsea Town Hall, London, 1977. The Transitional style of Brutalism, although designed in the 1960s, is seen here with the use of brick, bronzed glass and a more human scale.*

OVERLEAF: *Basil Spence, Kensington and Chelsea Town Hall, London, 1977. The form of the building, and the use of materials, was designed to complement the residential buildings around it as well as the brick built neo-classical library facing it from across the courtyard.*

YOUR LITTER PLEASE

On the Duchess of Bedford Walk elevation, essentially the back of the building, Spence created a beautiful interplay of overlapping forms, and so, rather than being a forgotten and functional service area, this is just as inviting and playful as the rest of the structure. Like Madin's Birmingham Library, Kensington and Chelsea appears like an inverted ziggurat, rising upward and outward from the ground. But the upper floors step back again, designed to remain complementary to the surroundings. Back on the south side, the twin volumes of the Great Hall and the Council Chamber present rather blank faces at the head of the quadrangle, the latter framed in concrete ribs at each of the canted corners which envelope the volume and form four squat columns which rise it above what was originally a pool but latterly has been converted into a flower bed.

Spence developed something of a speciality in civic building and during the 1960s and the early 1970s was the architect of choice for high quality and thoughtful solutions to the needs of British institutions such as his British Embassy in Rome (1959–71), an extraordinary set-piece in muscular concrete, and his British pavilion for the 1967 Montreal Exposition, full of the kind of angular geometry that would later inform his work at Kensington and the civic centre in Sunderland. A group whose specific and esoteric needs required careful handling was the Household Cavalry, whose proposed site for a new barracks was a sliver of land between Knightsbridge and Hyde Park. Spence won the commission most likely through his contacts, who included the War Office architect Donald Gibson and Lord Mountbatten. The consultation, planning and construction period mirrored that of the Embassy in Rome, beginning in 1959 and with several years of producing and revising plans in accordance with the brief and also the requirements of the planning authorities, with construction work finally commencing in 1967.

The solution that Spence proposed in order to accommodate stables, officers' barracks, riding school and parade ground, rifle range, canteens, storage rooms and messes, as well as a large number of living quarters, was a tower and podium arrangement, although the podium itself in this case consisted of several distinct, low-rise structures linked together and unified by a stylistic theme.

The existing barrack buildings had been designed by Thomas Henry Wyatt in 1878 and were essentially of a Neo-classical style, which had, by the early 1950s, reached such a poor condition that either major refurbishment or complete replacement was needed. The War Office chose the latter option and approved of Spence's designs, although the main feature of the scheme, his twenty-nine-storey tower, was questioned by the Royal Fine Arts Commission (RFAC) and the London County Council. Although the LCC had no planning jurisdiction over Crown property, they had developed a policy to keep buildings in the area of Hyde Park below 30m (100ft) so as to protect the integrity of the green space. Spence's tower was to be a little over 94m (308ft), clearly well above the edict, and so alternative designs were sought. The argument that Spence put forward, though, was that a lower-rise building such as a slab block would actually do more damage by reducing the aspect of older surrounding buildings and blocking out more light from the park. With Spence's passion for his project and weighty backing from the War Office, the RFAC eventually approved the tower.

This part of the project was one of the more distinctive blocks of post-war Britain, the closely banded horizontal floor beams tied together with exposed vertical columns which continued up around the recessed upper floor as fins to intersect over at the top. The podium buildings were subtly varied in height and surface texture to differentiate the various elements but united by the use of red brick and rough shuttered concrete. The horizontal concrete elements were gently arched in a design that strongly recalls Le Corbusier's Maison Jaoul and is a theme Spence had already used on a larger scale at Sussex University.

By the late 1970s, civic building began to move away from the brash aesthetic of Brutalism to follow the national trend towards something softer, more vernacular and less visually challenging.

Basil Spence, Hyde Park Cavalry Barracks, London, 1971. The tower dominates the site while the lower series of buildings recall Le Corbusier's Jaoul houses, an influence that returns in Spence's work at Sussex University.

The use of traditional materials such as brick, wood and tile replaced exposed concrete, hipped roofs replaced flat roofs, low-rise was favoured over high-rise. And so the 'Dutch barn' became the template for larger-scale structures in a homogenized form that would be the same from Sussex to Stirlingshire, and the universal use of which made it difficult to distinguish between a library and a county court, a leisure centre and a supermarket. Modernism had been the Zeitgeist and, while part of mainstream architectural thinking, it had been used liberally by local authorities to make their mark and create structures of distinction. Not all were successful, either visually or practically, but many were well considered in their design and use as well as sensitive to the buildings and landscapes around them. Some that have survived have even endeared themselves to the people who live by them and work in them.

OTHER NOTABLE BRUTALIST CIVIC BUILDINGS

United States Embassy, Grosvenor Square, London (Eero Saarinen, 1960): like a fortified slab, the classical proportions and use of staggered window mullions designed to blend with the Georgian facades around it.

Sunderland Town Hall and Civic Centre (Sir Basil Spence, Bonnington and Collins, 1970): like Kensington and Chelsea, another Transitional structure of elegant geometry and a synthesis of brown engineering bricks and reinforced concrete.

Trinity Car Park, Gateshead (demolished in 2010) (Rodney Gordon of the Owen Luder Partnership, 1969): another iconic Massive Brutalist building, perhaps because of its use in Mike Hodges's visceral thriller *Get Carter* rather than its architectural merits. It had a functional geometry and rough-cast elegance in keeping with its utilitarian function.

Trinity Car Park, Gateshead, undergoing demolition.

Portsmouth Central Library (Portsmouth City Architects Department, 1976): heavy bands of mosaic-clad horizontals with deep-set, ribbon windows and sculptural stairwells with a Lasdunesque service tower.

Crown Offices, Cardiff (Alex Gordon Partnership, 1980): on a grand scale and fortress-like, using Portland stone cladding the proportions are neo-classical, with its entrance colonnade, yet stripped and modern with projecting and recessed volumes.

Chapter 3

Educational Building

Amid the immediate post-war plans for the re-building of urban spaces and creating of new housing, a programme of school building was also launched. In Norfolk a comprehensive scheme was put in place with open competition and included a secondary school at Hunstanton in 1949, which was won by Alison and Peter Smithson. The Smithsons were the rising stars of British architecture, already finding themselves at odds with the older element of the CIAM and forming their own stance on architecture in society. Unlike Le Corbusier before them, the Smithsons' open-ended approach not only allowed for change but actively sought it, and almost demanded it.

Hunstanton School

This shifting aesthetic can be seen at work in their designs, both built and theoretical, throughout the 1950s and 1960s. When their plan for Hunstanton School was completed, British Modernism was experiencing a transition from the International Style to something more Scandinavian and humanist. Some of this architecture falls within the Early Brutalist form already identified, while some, like Hunstanton School, took its inspiration from Mies van der Rohe. The Smithsons, among their peers, had yet to be influenced by Le Corbusier's seminal *Unité d'Habitation*, the production period of which coincidentally almost exactly matched that of the school.

The building most likely to have inspired the design of Hunstanton School was Mies's Alumni Memorial Hall at the Illinois Institute of Technology (IIT) in Chicago (1945–47). It was built as part of a construction programme for the college, and utilised an axial plan and exposed steel structure. This was innovative at the time and had not been seen a great deal in modern architecture up to that point, steelwork generally being hidden behind walling and rendering. Here, though, Mies used structural steel as surface design, filled with brick and glass in a highly finished and symmetrical way.

While Mies may have been the inspiration for Hunstanton School, the Smithsons developed the design in their own way. The school was largely symmetrical in plan, the main building and teaching block forming a central space with an open box around it, creating voids within, garden courts cloistered safely in the enclosed space. The exposed skeletal steel frame, in-filled with brick or expanses of glass in a broadly symmetrical way, is strongly reminiscent of the IIT Alumni Memorial Hall, but here the finishes are rather different. Where Mies employed a highly polished finish, the Smithsons preferred to leave all the materials in their raw state, albeit still of high quality. The pre-cast concrete floor and ceiling slabs were not plastered and nor were interior brick walls. All the electrical and service conduits were visible, not hidden in ducting, but they were unobtrusive and no effort was made to emphasise these features.

Although it did not adopt the aesthetics that would later be associated with Brutalism, Hunstanton School was, nevertheless, the first

ALISON AND PETER SMITHSON (1928–93 AND 1923–2003)

Alison Smithson, née Gill, and her husband Peter played a pivotal role in the direction of British architecture during the second half of the twentieth century. They met at Durham University where both attended the school of architecture; they married in 1949, settling in the capital while working for the London County Council. Winning the competition to design a school at Hunstanton prompted them to establish their own practice and they continued to enter competitions for major projects, including Coventry Cathedral in 1951 and the redevelopment of Golden Lane in the City of London the following year. Their entry for the latter included photographs of the bomb-damaged Coventry, taking the place of central London, with serpentine slab blocks superimposed on them. It would be some years before their vision of urban housing would be realized, but in the meantime the couple co-founded a British radical splinter group of the CIAM in 1956 called Team 10. To the Smithsons, Team 10 was a vital forum for developing new architectural theories and, in particular, of urban planning. They also became involved with the Independent Group of artists and writers as a result of Peter's working at the Central School of Arts and Crafts alongside Eduardo Paolozzi who co-founded the organization. It was at this time that the concept of Brutalism took shape, chronicled by their fellow Independent Group member Reyner Banham, the critic and design historian. Also in 1956 the Smithsons worked with the Independent Group on the exhibition *This Is Tomorrow* at the Whitechapel Gallery, where they came into contact with Ernö Goldfinger and James Stirling. The exhibition set out to bring together art, architecture and cultural theory and tried to form relationships between the three that hitherto had not been achieved. The Smithsons' part of the exhibition, collaborating with Paolozzi and Nigel Henderson, placed objects they saw as central to the fulfilment of life into essential spaces: the patio and the pavilion.

One of their first major commissions after the exhibition was to design a new office complex for *The Economist* magazine on St James's Street, London (1964), but it was not until 1972 that their theories on urban planning found form in their housing megastructure at Poplar, the Robin Hood estate, a realization of their ribbon block first laid out in the Golden Lane proposal of 1952. This was Brutalism par excellence and placed its architects firmly alongside the likes of Goldfinger, Louis Kahn and Le Corbusier as masters of concrete.

ethically Brutalist building in Britain. It conformed to the principles laid down by its architects as the key attributes of modern building: the use of materials 'as found', left exposed and unadorned; the clearly visible structure, articulated throughout; and visual impact, immediately striking in its setting. This was a definitive break from the status quo in British Modernism, and as a commission independent from their work with the LCC it was an important first step for the Smithsons towards realising their Brutalist ideals. But in the meantime, Hunstanton stood opposed to the stripped, Scandinavian, Neo-classical style that dominated school and college building at the time. Its lines were so dramatic and new that it became something of a template for educational architecture during the post-war years. The design itself was not the most practically successful as the large expanses of glass created a greenhouse effect in the summer and left the building freezing in win-

ter. Other elements were more successful, however, such as the elevating of the classrooms above the noisy access corridors.

By the time Hunstanton School was completed the Smithsons had attended their first CIAM conference at Aix-en-Provence, forming associations with other younger-generation modern architects that would eventually lead to the formation of Team 10. Their meeting with Le Corbusier, whose work had taken a new direction in the late 1940s, gave them a stylistic, if not ideological, impetus that would permeate their work through the next two decades or so.

While primary and secondary education seemed to settle on either the Miesian structures loosely modelled on Hunstanton or the Scandinavian classicism of schools such as Sprites in Ipswich by Slater and Howard, it was with further and higher education that bolder and more avant-garde buildings found favour.

Domestic Trades College, Manchester

Leonard Howitt's building for the College, now part of the Metropolitan University's Hollings Campus, is a striking example of Early Period Brutalism. Known locally as 'The Toastrack', the main tower is a tapering, tent-like structure with concrete ribs that form parabolic arches at the top and then columns at the base which raise the building up at first-floor level. The design was intended to create differently sized interior spaces to accom-

RIGHT: Leonard Howitt, Manchester Domestic Trades College or 'Toastrack' (now Metropolitan University Hollings Campus), 1958. The main building showing tapering form and parabolic roof fins.

BELOW: Leonard Howitt, Manchester Domestic Trades College 'Fried Egg' (now Metropolitan University Hollings Campus), 1958. The 'fried egg' block with its graduated rotunda.

modate classes of varying size. The neighbouring, two-storey block with tailoring workshops was separated from the Toastrack to reduce noise pollution but maintain visual integrity, with tapering concrete ribs accentuating the window bays. An additional circular building, known appropriately enough as the 'Fried Egg', contained the library and refectories around a central exhibition hall.

The use of concrete and brick together on the exterior elevations, the narrow metal window mullions and the accentuation of load-bearing structures, give the building its lightness, emphasized by raising the main block from the ground, and draw clearly from the Scandinavian influences of the day.

LEFT: Leonard Howitt, Manchester Domestic Trades College (now Metropolitan University Hollings Campus), 1958. The dramatic sweep of the main tower, the interior spaces designed to contain varying class sizes.

BELOW: Leonard Howitt, Manchester Domestic Trades College (now Metropolitan University Hollings Campus), 1958. The three sections together including the central two-storey unit which originally housed the sewing machine shop with its distinctive concrete fins.

Dunelm House, University of Durham

The topography of Durham is naturally intersected by the River Wear, which snakes through the city in a whiplash curve. This forms a raised peninsula upon which sits the cathedral, a Romanesque masterpiece begun in the late eleventh century. The rocky cathedral promontory drops down to the river and then slopes up again on the opposite bank. In this challenging geography nestles the cluster of Brutalist concrete that is Dunelm House, the students' union building of Durham University, completed in 1966.

Architects Co-Partnership, Dunelm House, Durham University, 1966. View from the river, with Ove Arup's Kingsgate Bridge in the foreground.

Architects Co-Partnership, Dunelm House, Durham University, 1966. View from Kingsgate Bridge.

The structure was designed by the Architects Co-Partnership. As the name suggests, the firm had a collaborative ethos, with elder, more experienced partners giving joint project responsibility to younger junior architects. For Dunelm House, the team was led by Michael Powers, with Richard Raine as project architect; the engineering firm selected was Arup Associates and John Laing was contracted for the construction.

The choice of Arup was arguably inevitable and certainly had a degree of symmetry to it, given that the chosen site was right next to Ove Arup's Kingsgate Bridge, a concrete footbridge that vaults over the river gorge, connecting the cathedral peninsula with the newer part of the university at New Elvet. Indeed, the two structures, completed three years apart, work seamlessly together.

The brief for the building was to provide student leisure and entertainment facilities alongside separate staff club rooms. Structurally, the building comprises a series of interconnected concrete boxes, cast *in situ*, and this is clearly articulated on the exterior. The difficulties of the site, sloping as it does in two directions, were overcome by nestling the structure around a central spinal staircase, with spaces leading off to each side from landings. As you approach from the road, the building rises with the hill and rests on rock, while on the river side it cascades down to the water and is partly cantilevered on piles. On this elevation are broad ribbon windows affording unrivalled views of the river and cathedral. The roofs of the interlocking spaces slope in varying directions, giving the building a profile that undulates in tune with its surroundings.

All the walls are of rough shuttered concrete left 'as found', and the use of a special 'foam slag' lightweight concrete in addition to conventional concrete reduced the overall weight. Rather than using zinc or copper linings on the roofs, these were covered with bespoke pre-cast concrete tiles finished with a pink aggregate, laid in a slightly overlapping fashion to allow for expansion and contraction.

Leicester University

Leicester University boasts no fewer than three important buildings in the Brutalist manner, all built during the 1960s. The first of these is James Stirling and James Gowan's Engineering Building, completed in 1963, which has become iconic of both educational architecture but also post-war Modernism in general. Here we have an example of how Brutalist proportions and the interplay of asymmetrical volumes could work without the use of shuttered pre-cast concrete

RIGHT: *Stirling and Gowan, Engineering Faculty Building, Leicester University, 1963. The main tower shows influences from Expressionism, Russian Constructivism and the International Style in the use of materials and arrangement of volumes. (Image courtesy of Colin Brooks, Leicester University)*

BELOW: *Stirling and Gowan, Engineering Faculty Building, Leicester University, 1963. The glass, steel and brick of the tower rising over the saw-tooth roofline of the low-rise workshops. (Image courtesy of Colin Brooks, Leicester University)*

but with the more traditional materials of brick and glass around a steel internal structure.

The brief must have been something of a dream for a modern architect, a building the function of which dictates the use of starkly modern techniques, materials and styles, and Stirling brought to bear a startling combination of stylistic elements from Expressionism, Constructivism and the International Style. The need for a 30.5m (100ft) hydraulic supply on a constrained site meant that a tower was the obvious solution. The shape of this tower with its canted glass elevations recalls Bruno Taut's steel pavilion for the Leipzig fair of 1913 and perhaps Owen Williams's Boots warehouse at Beeston, Nottingham, of 1932, the combination of glass and brick being reminiscent of Frank Lloyd Wright's Johnson's Wax Co. research tower of 1950. It stands on four columns extending from the shaped stanchions above a brick-tile-faced, wedge-shaped cantilever, which, in turn, mirrors a similar projection on the north side of the lower tower. These projections have distinct resonances with Konstantin Melnikov's Rusakov Workers Club building in Moscow of 1928. The tower stood at a 45-degree angle to the low-rise block of engineering workshops, which did not escape Expressionist detailing with their jagged roof glazing.

Denys Lasdun contributed a great deal to educational building and at Leicester won the commission to design the Charles Wilson Building in 1961, which was completed in 1966. Named after the former Vice-Chancellor of the University, Sir Charles Wilson (1909–2002), it

---

JAMES STIRLING (1926–92)

Born in Glasgow, James Stirling became a key influential force in post-war architecture, but, like Spence and Lasdun, developed his own distinct stance and methodology. Although much of his work during the period is regarded as Brutalist, Stirling brought to bear a wide frame of reference from throughout architectural history, often within the same project, and thus could be regarded as a true post-modernist.

He studied architecture at Liverpool University under Colin Rowe between 1945 and 1950, after which he worked as an assistant for Lyons Israel Ellis before leaving to set up his own practice with fellow Lyons architect James Gowan. One of their first projects together was a group of houses at Ham Common, Richmond (1958), which, with its mix of brick and concrete elements, had stylistic links to Le Corbusier's Maison Jaoul, and achieved much critical acclaim. Among other early projects was the Engineering Faculty at Leicester, which brought elements of Expressionism and the International Style as well as references to Frank Lloyd Wright.

The partnership came to an end in 1963 and Stirling and Gowan went their separate ways, professionally if not stylistically. Notable structures from this early post-Gowan period were the History Faculty Library at Cambridge University and the Florey accommodation building at Oxford University, both of which introduced influences from Expressionism and the Finnish architect Alvar Aalto. Exploring preformed cladding elements in this period, Stirling utilized fibreglass at his training building for Olivetti at Haslemere in Surrey and pre-cast concrete at the Andrew Melville accommodation block at St Andrew's University. The latter of these two is pure Brutalism, although this was a title, like post-modernist, that Stirling himself rejected.

The 1970s and 1980s saw Stirling take on large-scale public buildings in Britain and abroad, notably in Germany where he designed three museums, earning him and his firm an international reputation. Towards the end of his life, Stirling's standing in the industry garnered him a knighthood, which he only reluctantly accepted, and, after his death, one of the most prestigious awards for architecture, the Stirling Prize, was named after him.

Denys Lasdun, Charles Wilson Building, Leicester University, 1966. The architect's characteristic horizontal emphasis and upper storeys with service tower a typical feature of his work. (Image courtesy of Colin Brooks, Leicester University)

was originally conceived with six storeys, but additional funding allowed for a further four which gave the building its unusual profile. The function of the building was to supply food and recreation in cafes, restaurants and common rooms and it was designed to cope with serving some 2,750 lunches a day to the staff and students. At the lower ground level all the food preparation, cooking and storage was located and everything made here was then taken to the upper floors via four service lifts in the central core. The first to the third floors were set aside for the students with serveries and self-service areas, the fourth floor contained a waitress-service restaurant and the fifth floor was a senior common room. The remaining four floors were contained in the narrower tower section with common rooms surmounted by a top-lit exhibition and recital space on the tenth floor.

The central core and its continuation in the form of the tower was constructed with in situ concrete, while the remaining elements, including columns, floor beams and staircase chambers, were pre-cast by a local contractor. The close proximity of the pre-cast elements meant that they could be delivered as needed by crane and put into position. In addition to this, the window frames were designed for fitting internally which meant that the whole building could be constructed without the need for scaffolding. At ground-floor level the north elevation extends out to form a general purpose hall with a snack bar; this was constructed with load-bearing brick walls with fair-faced brick elevations.

The total result is, when seen in the context of later buildings by Lasdun, a typical combination of stylistic and functional elements: the strong horizontal lines reflecting his interest in rock strata,

DENYS LASDUN (1914–2001)

Lasdun, being almost contemporary with Ernö Goldfinger, began his architectural career amid some of the first generation of Modernists, working with both Wells Coates and in the Tecton practice, with Berthold Lubetkin, becoming a member of MARS and the CIAM. At the time he joined Tecton in 1938, the celebrated Highpoint flats in Highgate were being joined by the neighbouring block Highpoint II, with its more plastic forms and the playful use of classical caryatids on the entrance portico. Although the Second World War intervened, during which Lasdun served in the Royal Engineers, he returned to Tecton to work on the Hallfield housing estate in Paddington, where the slab blocks show a significant similarity to Highpoint II. After completing Hallfield, he left Tecton to form a partnership with his partner on the project, Lindsay Drake, and was joined by E. Maxwell Fry, who had been a key player in the British inter-war Modern Movement. During the 1950s Lasdun began to develop alternative theories on mass housing from the existing trend of slab blocks, which took shape at Bethnal Green in London with the 'cluster' blocks, such as Sulkin House and the more infamous Keeling House. The latter became an example to be used by both sides of the argument for and against modern architecture's role in solving housing problems: on the one side because of its unique arrangement of spaces providing both privacy and insulation from noise as well as community spirit, and on the other because its hard-edged Modernist profile contrasted sharply with the existing Victorian terraces around it, which was misinterpreted as soulless and lacking in character. Keeling – one of the earliest modernist post-war mass housing projects – became the subject of a heated debate in the early 1990s when its fate hung in the balance between demolition and rejuvenation. The latter course was taken and the building preserved but as a luxury apartment block, contrasting sharply with its roots.

Much of Lasdun's post-war work involved large organizations, such as colleges and universities, where his interest in geology, and in particular rock strata, became more apparent. This phase began with the Royal College of Physicians building at Regent's Park and evolved through larger-scale projects such as the University of East Anglia and the School of Oriental and African Studies (SOAS) in London, which demonstrated his ability to create megastructures of great integrity and style. His commission for the National Theatre on London's South Bank, a little up-river from the Royal Festival Hall, was a masterclass in rough, shuttered concrete and great attention to the needs of the brief. Also visible at the National Theatre is the influence of Frank Lloyd Wright, from whom Lasdun drew more inspiration than the luminaries of the first generation European Modernists, and when one looks at Falling Water in Pennsylvania, for example, the parallels become clear. One of the last Brutalist buildings to be completed in Britain, Lasdun's IBM headquarters next to the National Theatre (1982) came at a time of transition in British architecture as the brashness of Brutalism gave way to the emerging neo-vernacular. While the strong horizontal lines here mirror those of the neighbouring theatre, there is the tempering presence of brick, heralding a return to traditional materials and forms.

Lasdun never regarded himself as a Brutalist, although his work between 1959 and the early 1980s will forever be grouped in this genre because, stylistically if not philosophically, the buildings captured the predominant visual theme of the period.

the recessed ribbon windows, the service core and cuboid service towers, and the intersecting vertical staircase towers. It is a bold and considered design where form follows function but allows for a pleasing interplay of volumes, and a grounded and solid concrete form that is saved from being overweight by the use of projecting floor beams which allow the structure to float in its space.

The engineering consultants for the Charles Wilson Building were Arup Associates, which must have played a part in their winning a commission to design an arts and humanities building nearby. The Attenborough Tower, named after Frederick Attenborough, Principal of Leicester University College from 1931 to 1951 and father to Richard and David, was a cluster block intended as part of a series of three. At 52m (170ft) it was one of the tallest buildings in the city and contained some 270 offices and tutorial rooms as well as two large lecture theatres and, in a lower floor area, a film theatre and the central service core containing a paternoster lift to access each floor.

The construction was of concrete frame cast in situ with floors, walls and exterior panels in pre-cast concrete. The central service core is of a polygonal form with three blocks projecting out. Each of these has canted corners and three elevations with three bays of windows. The profile of the building is very tactile, which became something of an Arup trademark, the window frames angled outwards towards the bottom, designed to assist draught-free ventilation but also serving to add texture, the geometric nature of which recalls the Expressionism of Melnikov and Frank Lloyd Wright.

Royal College of Physicians

In 1960 work began on a rather different structure by Denys Lasdun at Regent's Park. His building for the Royal College departed from the horizontal ribbed block format of the Charles Wilson Building and St James's Place and was rather more heavily influenced by Le Corbusier. At first glance there are superficial similarities to the Villa Savoye, with its floating white box, and also to the monastery at La Tourette with its heavy rectangular volumes. Closer inspection reveals an L-shaped building with a brick-faced administration block, its ribbon windows facing out over Albany Street and enclosing a courtyard on the park side. The ground floor elements are faced in dark blue brick

Arup Associates, Attenborough Tower, Leicester University, 1970. The cluster block formed from three towers arranged around a central service core, the exterior with surface texture created by angling the windows out. (Image courtesy of Colin Brooks, Leicester University)

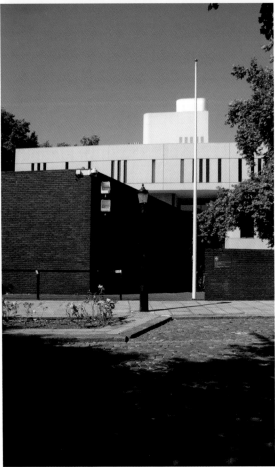

and the central block, cantilevered at first floor and faced in white Candiolo porcelain mosaic tile, is surmounted with the Lasdun trademark service tower. The seemingly random placement of narrow vertical strip windows on the central block enhances its ambiguous nature and on the side elevations are curiously, and somewhat prophetically, reminiscent of DNA fingerprints.

Internally the building is divided into three main spaces on the upper floors, a two-storey library, which could also be used for meetings with space for up to 400 people, a dining room with seating for 200 and a reception room which overlooks St Andrew's Place. Between these last two spaces is a hydraulic partition which can be lifted to create a space running the width of the building. On the ground floor are the administrative offices, committee rooms, a small lecture theatre seating fifty and common rooms which open out on to a garden. Projecting southward from the ground floor foyer is a low, brick-faced structure of pyramidal form which contains a lecture theatre for 300 as well as equipment for translation, colour CCTV and accommodation for the lecturer, allowing it to be used independently from the main building if need be. The construction was of in situ prestressed concrete walls with pre-cast floor slabs around a central group of columns and the roof of pre-cast concrete

OPPOSITE ABOVE: Denys Lasdun and Partners, Royal College of Physicians, Regents Park, London, 1964. Entrance front facing Regents Park, the building 'floating' on slender columns.

OPPOSITE BELOW: Denys Lasdun and Partners, Royal College of Physicians, Regents Park, London, 1964. The St.Andrew's Place elevation with characteristic service tower. The arrangement of windows curiously reminiscent of a DNA sequence 'ladder'.

BELOW: Denys Lasdun and Partners, Royal College of Physicians, Regents Park, London, 1964. The North West corner with entrance foyer recessed and faced in grey brick, the stair tower a Lasdun feature that would appear in later buildings.

slabs laid on steel beams. The interior spaces used some of the finest materials available, including white Sicilian marble from Tuscany, polished manganese bronze, East African muninga wood and Tasmanian oak.

The Royal College of Physicians, in addition to the day-to-day educational life that it contained, also had at its heart a very traditional aspect, steeped in centuries-old ceremony which had to continue in Lasdun's new building. One of the key elements of the brief was to house the Censor's room, the interior walls of which would be lined with seventeenth-century wood panelling taken from the previous College building in Trafalgar Square, which had, in turn, used the panelling from a still earlier building in Warwick Lane. Lasdun placed the Censor's room on the first floor

overlooking the garden and integrated the old, traditional materials within his new modern framework. As if this were not challenge enough, the site of the College had been occupied by a building by John Nash and surrounded by yet more buildings by him. Lasdun managed to integrate his college extremely well by a careful choice of materials and finishes as well as design. The white tile exterior of the main block was designed to blend in with the Neo-classical stuccoed facades around it, and the blue brick angular lecture block was designed to mirror the hipped slate roofs of those same neighbouring buildings. Though uncompromisingly modern and bringing elements of the International Style and Brutalism, the Royal College of Physicians provided a highly traditional institution with new premises which has accommodated its needs into the new millennium, while reflecting and enhancing the architectural heritage around it.

Cambridge University

Two architectural practices working in Cambridge tackled student accommodation at two colleges in similar ways. Built within three years of each other, Powell and Moya's Cripps Building (1967) in St John's and Arup Associates' graduate housing for Corpus Christi (1964) have some obvious stylistic resonances with each other and both, like Lasdun's Royal College of Physicians, had the difficult task of working their Brutalist profiles into a geography crammed with history and tradition. One must not forget, though, that the sprawling campuses of Cambridge and Oxford had taken hundreds of years to develop and grow, evolving through many stylistic periods. Modernism, therefore, was simply the next period style and so should not have been any more incongruous than Neo-classicism was along with Gothic. In addition, these somewhat cloistered, cerebral environments seem to be ready made to accept the bold and the *avant-garde* in architectural terms.

Cambridge is, indeed, a city of contrasts where period styles mix with starkly modern structures, seeming to coexist quite happily. Powell and Moya's Cripps building could not have been placed in a more idyllic setting than it was, stretching ribbon-like through parkland right up to the banks of the Cam. Its neighbours were, to the north, Sir Edwin Lutyens's Benson Court of Magdalene College, to the south, Hutchinson's Neo-Gothic New Court of 1830, and to the west, the twelfth-century School of Pythagoras. And so Cripps had much to live up to. Indeed, the external framework and exposed floor beams, as well as the purposely undulating roof line, had a great deal of the Perpendicular Gothic about them.

The structure zigzags across the site, forming separate courts and making the best advantage of the sun. There were four storeys plus a penthouse containing no fewer than 200 undergraduate rooms in all as well as a common room, three squash courts and several workshops.

The construction comprised reinforced concrete, L-shaped columns forming the outer skeleton and housing service ducts, with concrete floor slabs, the edges of which were exposed and sand-blasted to a smooth finish. The window frames were of bronze, with polished white concrete mullions, external cladding on the columns, and walls of Portland stone. Internally, the building had a virtually free plan so partitions were of non-structural concrete finished with rough textured plaster. The clean lines of the interior spaces were enhanced with an underfloor heating system, supplemented with fan-assisted storage heaters incorporated in the window seats.

About half a mile away Arup Associates' graduate housing block, the George Thompson Building, was on a much smaller scale, but nevertheless just as striking with its elevations accentuating the polished concrete framework. Here the location is more isolated, tucked away in the western suburbs; the design was intended to extend and supplement the existing Leckhampton House, a red-brick Victorian villa by

William Marshall and adopted by Corpus Christi to house research fellows and graduate students.

The George Thompson Building provided room for an additional twenty-eight students with rooms for three married couples. The space was arranged in two blocks off-set from each other and linked by staircases and services, the position and profile of the building designed in sympathy with the site and the existing trees as well as Leckhampton House itself. The external structure uses a series of H-frame pre-cast concrete sections finished with a limestone aggregate designed to maintain its appearance through weathering. The linking stair and service block is a staggered section with overlapping red-brick-faced walls reflecting those of the neighbouring villa.

On the ground floor a recreation room took up almost all of the southern block, while the northern block comprised a laundry, boiler room and cloakrooms. Accommodation, then, was confined to the first, the second and the third floors.

Arup Associates had plenty of experience with both concrete and with multi-storey developments, having recently completed the Point Royal

Powell and Moya, Cripps Building, St.John's College, Cambridge, 1967. The zigzag structure contrasts sharply with its parkland setting but the human scale and interplay of vertical and horizontal forms help to break up its profile. (Image courtesy of Steve Cadman)

flats at Bracknell, and so with their design for Corpus Christi the project architect Philip Dowson produced a design which had to overcome problems of concrete weathering in the British climate as well as issues of the cloistering effect of apartment living. Indeed, this latter point was one that the College was keen to avoid while maintaining a sense of place and community.

A third building at Cambridge, completed in the same year as the Cripps building, was James Stirling's History Faculty, which followed on from his engineering building at Leicester with a similarly Expressionist style. Here we find the same combination of geometric, crystalline, glass forms retained by brick-faced sections. Stirling won the commission to build through a limited competition and his concept, unlike those of the other entrants, brought the library and teaching spaces together by placing the reading room within the L-shaped embrace of the seminar and administration block. The original

siting of the building had to be adjusted as the parcel of land earmarked for the project was changed before construction began. This was overcome by simply turning the proposed building on its axis by 90 degrees and, as it was designed to be approached from several directions, this did not present any undue difficulties.

The reading room accommodated up to 300 people with space for just over 1,120sq.m (12,000sq.ft) of shelving beneath a double skin of glass within a tent-like steel framework fanning out between the upright blocks. Here Stirling placed a greater emphasis on the glass, sculpted into geometric forms and scarcely contained within the brick-faced end elevations and stair tower. As at Leicester, there are resonances with Expressionism and Constructivism, particularly Melnikov's Soviet pavilion for the 1925 Paris Exposition. But also there was a Scandinavian influence, most clearly seen in the

fan-shaped lecture theatre at the Otaniemi Institute of Technology by Alvar Aalto, completed in 1964, the year work began on Stirling's building at Cambridge. He adopted a similar approach with his Florey Building at Oxford, which almost looks like the mould from which the Cambridge History Faculty was cast.

By placing the largest and most heavily populated spaces at lower levels, Stirling created a stepped or terraced profile to the L block and he placed the 'double-barrelled' stair tower off-centre on the north elevation. There is an exciting undulation and variety in the forms, but the consistency of the glass and brick prevents the result from being messy. It is unified, confident and coherent. Seen from above, the clarity of the design is most apparent, as is the crystalline form. From this vantage point there is a clear enunciation of the reading room's focus, dictated by the brief itself, a central point from which the whole room

could be surveyed, a command post positioned at the apex of the glass tent, and this again mirrors the internal focus of Aalto's OIT building.

One concept inextricably bound with Brutalist architecture is that of the megastructure, a large and complex unit, sometimes containing a variety of internal functions. Here the dictates of Le Corbusier communicated most readily, embodied in the Unité d'Habitation, with its complete range of community facilities. New university building in Britain presented one of the best opportunities for architects to conceive and build megastructures. At Cambridge, Denys Lasdun did just that with his New Court for Christ's College, completed in 1970, right at the heart of the Massive period. The design was originally intended as the first phase in a residential and sports complex, although the second phase was never built.

The site was fairly confined, nonetheless, wedged between King Street to the north and the Gothic buildings around the third courtyard. Lasdun's structure rises like a concrete mountain range, with a profile that became characteristic of his work, the service towers rising up and standing like sentinels over the roof terraces. Here there is more cloistering of the structure, although perhaps the architect could be pardoned for this given the constraints of the site. The King Street facade, such as it was, originally appeared much like that of his SOAS library, explored below, a concave and rather austere structure akin to a fortified wall defending a town. This has more recently been filled in with neo-Victorian facades which have somewhat lessened the impact of New Court; although, unable to cover the undulating roof line in concrete looming above, this new frontage does keep the eye at street level and remains in scale with the surrounding period buildings.

James Stirling, History Faculty Library, Cambridge University, 1967. A great glass canopy spread out between an L-shaped block clad in red brick. Like Leicester's Engineering tower there are strong resonances of Expressionism, particularly in the emphasis on geometry in the glass and steel elements.

London University

Lasdun designed two buildings for the University of London, the briefs for which tackle their commission in similar ways, if only at a superficial level. These were the Institute of Education and Law (IEL) building and the School of Oriental and African Studies (SOAS) library, both in Bloomsbury. Due to their sheer scale, especially within the context of the surrounding buildings, they may both be termed megastructures, which, in central London, is no mean feat.

The brief for the Institute of Education dates from 1960, although construction did not commence until 1975, with completion four years later. The result was a massive, eight-storey structure with an 800m (875yd)-long facade down Bedford Way, the entrance front with courtyard plaza in Woburn Square facing the SOAS library. The building comprises huge expanses of glass, framed by concrete forms, including Lasdun's trademark service towers launching upwards from the roof line, and exposed staircases on the west elevation cascading forward like great waterfalls, drawing inspiration from the concrete virtuoso Louis Kahn, the Estonian-born American architect. Like New Court at Cambridge, the IEL building was intended as the first phase in a larger plan for the University, but, coming as it did towards the end of the Transitional period when the Brutalist aesthetic was giving way to other influences, further clearance of Bloomsbury's older buildings was considered too much.

PREVIOUS PAGE: *Denys Lasdun, New Court, Christ's College, Cambridge, 1970. A Massive period megastructure in a confined setting with trademark service towers and rock strata profile. (Image courtesy of Debbie Soon)*

OPPOSITE: *Denys Lasdun and Partners, School of Oriental and African Studies Library, London, 1975. The Torrington Square facades have a simple elegance with bands of concrete and tinted glass within black metal mullions showing influences from the International Style.*

BELOW: *Denys Lasdun and Partners, Institute of Education, London, 1977. On the Woburn Square elevation the massive service towers appear to stand like sentinels above the expanses of glass.*

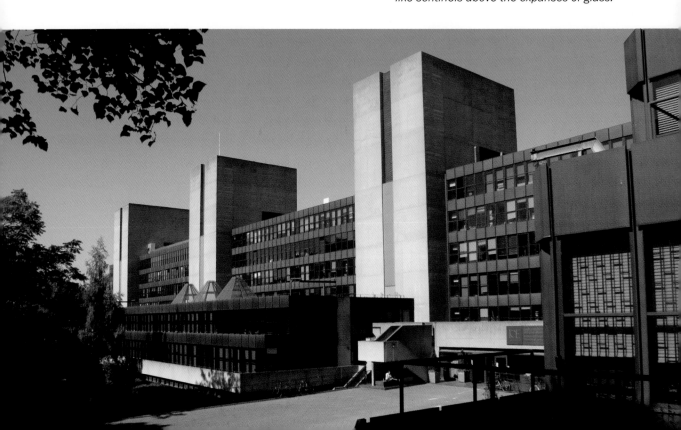

ABOVE: *Denys Lasdun and Partners, Institute of Education, London, 1977. The masterly use of sculptural forms in concrete is softened by the bronzed metal window casements, the characteristic stair tower reminiscent of Louis Khan.*

OPPOSITE: *Denys Lasdun and Partners, Institute of Education, London, 1977, Bedford Way elevation where concrete massing at street level provides plenty of incident, depth and changes in light.*

University of East Anglia

Perhaps Lasdun's most ambitious university project, and one of the most celebrated Brutalist megastructures in Britain, was the UEA in Norwich. Completed at the same time as New Court, Cambridge, the similarity between the two is marked and by no means coincidental. Striking also is the similarity between these projects and one of the most significant housing schemes in Europe, the Siedlung Halen at Berne in Switzerland by the Atelier 5 group, completed in 1960. In all three we see stepped terraces of concrete units accentuated with frameworks of concrete floor, wall and ceiling slabs forming *brise-soleil*, rising upwards on gently sloping or undulating landscapes with planting around. While Siedlung Halen and, to a lesser extent, New Court nestle within mature wooded environs, UEA rather

dominates its site. However, Lasdun achieved a successful union between his scheme and the landscape by creating what he referred to as 'strata', gently undulating levels with interconnected spaces, arranging modules at regular angles of 45 or 90 degrees, so that the whole appears to grow out of the landscape like a crystalline mountain.

The brief called for minimal division between disciplines and so Lasdun arranged the teaching spaces along an embracing line with residential blocks standing around the central 'harbour' and with views of the sloping landscape down towards the River Yare. The structures were of pre-cast concrete in stepped, pyramidal floors surmounted by cuboid stair and service towers. At UEA there were no earlier buildings to contend with or complement, as there were at Cambridge and London, but yet there is a strong sense that the landscape itself informed the arrangement of these forms and was reflected in the contours of the scheme.

ABOVE: Denys Lasdun, East Anglia University, 1970. Lasdun's interest in rock strata is apparent here in the accommodation blocks of pyramidal form with strong horizontal banding, surmounted by typical service towers. (Image courtesy of East Anglia University)

LEFT: Denys Lasdun, East Anglia University, 1970. A concrete mega-structure that seems to rise out of the ground like a crystalline mountain range. (Image courtesy of East Anglia University)

*Denys Lasdun, East Anglia University, 1970.
The crystalline imagery of the scheme is emphasized
by 'V' shaped gutters and the expanses of glass
which reflect back the landscape and temper the
impact of so much concrete. (Image courtesy of
East Anglia University)*

Liverpool University

Lasdun continued his educational work when his practice took on the new sports centre for Liverpool University in 1967. As with the Charles Wilson Building at Leicester, Lasdun and Partners teamed with Arup Associates as structural engineers and the architect team was headed by Stefan Kuszell. Standing on the corner of Bedford Street North and Oxford Street, the centre is at the heart of the University complex, close to the student union and Basil Spence's Sydney Jones Library. The profile facing Oxford Street is striking and distinctive with its row of pre-cast concrete columns drilling into the paving slabs and steeply raked at a 72-degree angle. This feature is repeated on the opposite elevation and between them is a perfectly arranged sports facility, including a swimming pool, four squash courts, a dojo, a multi-purpose hall and climbing wall, among other offices and service rooms. Built for the newly established Department of Physical Education, the facility also served the several undergraduate sporting clubs, catering to some 4,000 students with enough space to accommodate around 200 at any time. The centre was divided into two on either side of a central core. On the ground floor the 37m (120ft) main hall was marked out for tennis, badminton and netball, with a plant room with offices and service areas on the other side. Between these two spaces the central core contained a studio, training room, changing rooms and store rooms. At first-floor level the swimming pool was elevated above the plant room, while above the main hall is a clear storey with a climbing wall at the east end and in the central core here the dojo, changing rooms, offices and a buffet, with staircases at the east and the west end. At the second-floor level the clear storey continues above the swimming pool and hall with four squash courts in the central core, flanked on the south with a viewing gallery overlooking the pool.

The structure comprises reinforced concrete walls and floors supported by pairs of reinforced concrete columns, the central core providing the

Denys Lasdun and Partners, Liverpool University Sports Centre, Oxford Street, Liverpool, 1967. Here the dramatic angled elevation is seen to its best effect, the supporting columns plunging into the pavement.

stable base from which to hang the roof span and tie together the large hall and the swimming pool spaces. The pool itself was designed as a separate structure within the envelope of the south half of the centre, resting on the first-floor slab and so isolating it from any movement in the total structure to protect it from cracking.

The exterior has broad, double-glazed windows along each of the side elevations behind the raked columns, while the gable ends have pre-cast concrete facing slabs over lattice steelwork and the whole structure projects out at first-floor level on all sides, giving the impression that it hovers over the ground between the supporting fingers of the colonnades. Interior walls are faced in brick and tile and the floors are tiled or clad in hardwood strips. More recently, the building has been extended on the south elevation with a steel-framed structure that reflects the elements of the original facade with a similar series of raked struts, this time in painted metal.

Close to the sports centre, in what is now known as the University Precinct, a square of land bordered by Bedford Street South, are two further buildings which form something of a phalanx of Massive-period Brutalism, being constructed between 1964 and 1967. It is a feast of rough-cast concrete and heavy volumes, with an emphasis on scale and surface texture.

Both were designed by the same architect, Brian Westwood, commencing construction in 1962 – the Law, Social Sciences and Modern Languages building on Cypress Street and the Arts Library on Bedford Street South. There is a unity of form between the two with a weighty piano nobile jutting out above a dark brick plinth at ground floor.

The Law building was a cuboid block with a distinctive, slatted, upper level, forming mullions around the narrow strip windows. Like many Massive Brutalist buildings, it has an ambiguous and almost austere facade, but is saved from off-putting severity by the landscaping and planting around it, which creates an inviting and sophisticated promenade that has not dated in the intervening years.

Westwood's Arts Library was intended to work in unison with Spence's Sydney Jones Library although its use has since changed. The reinforced concrete cladding was arranged to form patterns in sections, while the longer and narrower structure rises gently at each end and forms a bridge over the centre supported by narrow columns and affords views through the building to the other side.

Basil Spence's contribution to Liverpool University's campus began construction in 1974 and was completed in 1976. Like his Kensington and Chelsea Town Hall, the Sydney Jones library is an important example of Transitional Brutalism. There is still a strong use of concrete visible on the exterior and an interplay of heavy volumes, with an emphasis on the meeting of horizontal and vertical. The use of dark red brick as a predominant facing material with deeply recessed, tinted, ribbon windows in dark bronze frames within a low-rise scheme on a more

Denys Lasdun and Partners, Liverpool University Sports Centre, Oxford Street, Liverpool, 1967. The entrance elevation with central service tower raised above the roof.

Denys Lasdun and Partners, Liverpool University Sports Centre, Oxford Street, Liverpool, 1967. On Oxford Street itself the raked columns support the projecting first floor and form a sheltered walkway.

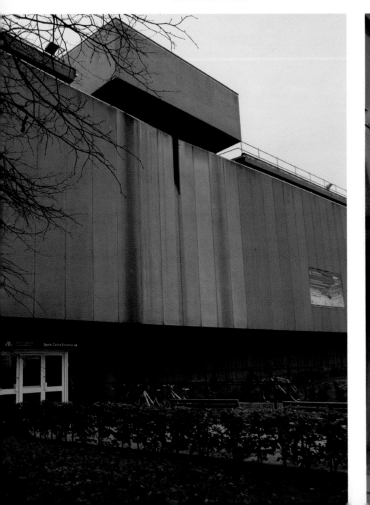

ABOVE: *Basil Spence, Sydney Jones Library, Liverpool University, 1976. Spence's use of concrete and brick as well as the strong horizontal emphasis show influences from Frank Lloyd Wright.*

BELOW: *Basil Spence, Sydney Jones Library, Liverpool University, 1976. The interior bays articulated on the outside, cantilevered on reinforced concrete double columns.*

human scale provides a clear indication of the changing mood in modern architecture and the search for a vernacular style.

But this is still an uncompromisingly modern building. The play of volumes is highly reminiscent of Frank Lloyd Wright, particularly (although on a smaller scale) the Robie House of 1909 and Falling Water of 1939, but also, like Stirling's Leicester engineering block, has links to the Johnson's Wax building in the use of materials. The Sydney Jones Library is almost like an enlarged 'prairie' house with the long, overhanging eaves, horizontal emphasis and seemingly low roof line. To the front elevation the stair tower frames the entrance and projects outward, intersecting the exposed floor and roof beams, continuing up above the roof line in a cluster of four towers and faced in brick. At each end of the window strips are brick-faced cuboid projections which continue on the south elevation where the first and the second storey are cantilevered outward, supported by double beams of rectangular section. Here the brick-faced cubes accent internal bays, each with a tiny central window to provide enough natural light without risking damage to the materials inside.

This side of the building has a strong sense of fortification, a theme that can be found in Spence's other projects, as at Queen Anne's Gate and the British Embassy in Rome.

The post-war period in Britain saw a renaissance in education which encompassed the comprehensive system and the development of new universities and a drive to increase the number of students continuing their education through to higher levels. This drove a building programme for schools and colleges throughout the country, and, while it seems that either Miesian or Scandinavian influences tended to predominate in school building, Brutalism played a strong role in shaping the landscapes of higher and further education. The campuses of colleges and universities, either new or long established, were fertile ground for challenging and exciting building and some of Britain's key practitioners, Stirling, Lasdun and Spence among them, were at the vanguard of this exciting field in British architecture.

OTHER NOTABLE BRUTALIST EDUCATIONAL BUILDINGS

Andrew Melville Hall, St Andrew's University, Scotland (James Stirling, 1968): a truly Brutalist concrete structure, if not megastructure; in spite of the stance of its architect, the 270 rooms are clearly articulated with exterior ribbing which gives the V-shaped block a hard-edged, sculptural quality.

Brunel University Lecture Theatre (Richard Sheppard, 1972): an extraordinary, bold and iconically Massive Brutalist structure with projecting volumes, sculptural forms and ocean-liner imagery; used as a location in Stanley Kubrick's dystopian masterpiece *A Clockwork Orange*.

New Museums Building, Cambridge (Arup Associates, 1974): in the Massive tradition, this imposing structure dominates its setting by sheer brute force and houses the Zoology and the Metallurgy Departments, comprising a three-storey block raised above a pedestrian deck and punctuated with a canted tower.

Great Hall and Hugh Owen Building, Aberystwyth University (Percy Thomas Partnership, 1975): university building on a grand scale and with elegant, modernist interplay of volumes and wide expanses of glass.

Richard Sheppard (Sheppard Robson & Partners), Brunel University lecture theatre, 1972. An archetypal Brutalist structure with chunky proportions, interplay of volumes and rough shuttered concrete. (Image courtesy of Sally Trussler, Brunel University)

Chapter 4

Commercial Building

The commercial sector in Britain was also experiencing something of a renaissance as the rapid development of a consumer society was under way, while business, industry and financial services flourished in a widening world market. This meant that there was money to spend on building for work and commerce within a sector that was eager to show that it was ahead of its time, forward thinking and progressive. Modernism, therefore, was the style of choice, but here, more than in any other aspect of British architecture, there seems to have been a stronger division between the two main schools, which were loosely Miesian and Corbusian. In North America it was Ludwig Mies van der Rohe who led the way with commercial building, naturally enough as he had emigrated there in 1937. In Chicago and New York the glass and steel tower or slab and podium became the accepted corporate style during the immediate post-war period and this had its impact on British building as well. Here buildings such as Gollins Melvin and Ward's Castrol House on Marylebone Road (1959) and Sydney Kaye's Euston Tower on the Euston Road (1970) followed the Miesian edict and were successful examples of their type, surviving largely unaltered into the twenty-first century. On the other side of the coin, though, some of Britain's most innovative and challenging Brutalist structures may be found in the commercial category.

Gollins, Melvin and Ward, Castrol House, Marylebone Road, London, 1959. A classic Miesian glass and steel tower and podium.

The Economist Building

One of Alison and Peter Smithson's most celebrated projects, and one of only a few commercial structures the couple built, was that for *The Economist* newspaper on London's St James's Street, completed in 1964. A number of factors set this building apart from the Smithsons' other work in the mid-1960s, namely scale, materials and form, all of which combined to create an elegantly proportioned cluster block, which presents one of the more restrained examples of early Massive period Brutalism. Tying all this together was the concept of the plaza, a raised platform counteracting the downward slope of St James's Street and on which the three blocks stood. Through this visitors, residents and workers could walk on a meandering route between St James's Street and Bury Street with tantalizing views through to the spaces beyond.

The project was initiated by the then chairman of The Economist Newspaper Ltd, Sir Geoffrey Crowther, who wanted to build a new London headquarters with a penthouse for himself on the top floor. The Smithsons were recommended by Leslie Martin, but Crowther also sought an alternative proposal from George, Trew and Dunn. But in 1960 the Smithsons won the contract and work began. The design incorporated a 53m (174ft), seventeen-floor tower block set back from the main street and containing the magazine's offices. A smaller block was set in front of this on St James's Street containing shops and a bank, while a third intermediate block nestled to the side of the main tower on Bury Street next to Boodle's gentleman's club and containing apartments.

OPPOSITE: Sydney Kaye, Euston Tower, Euston Road, London, 1970, following the Miesian tradition more than ten years after Castrol House showing the lasting appeal of this style.

The unifying theme between the towers was the chamfered corners, which draw the eye into the cloistered spaces within on the raised plaza, the ribbed external framework and the travertine panels set within the exterior faces. These elements combine to give the cluster a distinctive appearance which, rather than being at odds with the surrounding buildings, complements and reflects them while remaining solid and business-like, befitting its function.

Alison and Peter Smithson, The Economist Buildings, St James's St, London, 1964. The St. James's Street elevation with the shorter bank building at the front with Economist tower behind.

■ Commercial Building

The Smithsons' approach was imbued with their theories on town planning, although it did not seem at the time, or even now, to be as harshly unyielding as their Brutalist manifesto. The result is a perfect synthesis of form and function in concert with its much older and smaller-scale surroundings. To overcome the issue of scale, the Smithsons arranged the three blocks so that the tallest was set back and becomes, from certain angles on St James's Street, invisible, while the smallest block at the front remained proportionate with its neighbours. To assist the blocks' integration, the adjacent wall of Boodle's was refaced with a new bay window designed to match The Economist towers.

ABOVE: *Alison and Peter Smithson, The Economist Buildings, St James's Street, London, 1964. The choice and quality of materials and attention to detail soften the impact of the building, which has aged well.*

LEFT: *Alison and Peter Smithson, The Economist Buildings, St James's Street, London, 1964, Bury Street elevation showing the third tower with accommodation, the unified design allowing the cluster to work as a whole despite the different uses of each block.*

The third and narrowest block was then positioned beside Boodle's and contained, in addition to the private apartments on the upper floors, further accommodation for the club, including that reserved for ladies.

Looking more closely at the three buildings on their plaza, some modulation in their appearance becomes apparent. The front block with its ground-floor-level shops gives access to the bank on the first floor in a piano nobile that has a significantly taller bay of windows, the upper levels accommodating offices with fenestration in keeping with that of the other two blocks. The taller block housing The Economist offices was built around a central core with reinforced concrete slab floors, allowing uninterrupted space all round and consequently uninterrupted facades.

In his critique of the project for the Architectural Review in 1965, Gordon Cullen had much to praise although he felt that the taller tower imposed too much on the surroundings, particularly when seen from St James's Park. But the concept of dividing the functions of the scheme into three blocks instead of having only one was a key innovation which was considered the most favourable option. The most likely alternative, had another architect been selected, would have been the classic slab and podium arrangement and one could easily imagine a structure resembling Castrol House, which, while being highly fashionable, would not have integrated with its environment as well and neither would it have stood the test of time as the Smithsons' solution has.

Alison and Peter Smithson, The Economist Buildings, St James's Street, London, 1964, showing the plaza between the blocks with its inviting and cloistered walkway between St James's Street and Bury Street.

Alison and Peter Smithson, The Economist Buildings, St James's Street, London, 1964. Though a solid mass, the canted corners reduce the impact of the blocks amid much older buildings while the recessed ground-floor levels behind narrow pilotis lessen their visual weight.

Preston Bypass Service Station

In 1958 the dawn of a new era in transport came. The building of the Preston bypass laid the foundations of Britain's coming motorway network. The bypass would eventually become part of the country's longest and busiest motorway, the M6, which, by 1965, stretched from Barthomley in Cheshire all the way to Lancaster. The section between Preston and Lancaster opened in that year boasted one of the most modern and visually arresting service stations in the entire network. Forton Services by T.P. Bennett & Sons could be seen for many miles with its unique 'mushroom' tower standing 20m (66ft). Rank, the owners of the site, foresaw the M6 growing as a major arterial route between London and Edinburgh, with Lancaster standing at approximately the halfway mark, making it the ideal location for a comprehensive service station and stop-over for both north- and south-bound travellers.

Rank commissioned T.P. Bennett & Sons to design and build the scheme, leaving the decision-making to the project architects Bill Galloway and Ray Anderson. Their concept involved two flat-roofed units on each side of the carriageway, linked by an enclosed, glazed footbridge. The extraordinary tower stood on the north-bound side above a polygonally-shaped ground-floor unit with ribbon windows all round. This part of the structure was originally intended to be over 30m (98ft) tall, but had 10m (33ft) shaved off the height to meet local planning restrictions. The steel structure was clad in pre-cast concrete, with a cantilevered hexagonal gallery perched on top. This 'Pennine Tower', as it was called, provided visitors with a restaurant to seat 120 and a sun deck above. Ribbon windows, which cantilevered from the outer walls, gave visitors all round, unparalleled, panoramic views wherever they sat at tables. These ribbon windows were repeated on the ground floor podium, covering nearly all the elevations with an emphasis on the motorway-facing side.

T P Bennett & Son (Bill Galloway and Ray Anderson), Forton Services, Lancaster, 1966. Seen from the southbound carriageway the full impact of the tower with its polygonal podium.

T P Bennett & Son (Bill Galloway and Ray Anderson), Forton Services, Lancaster, 1966. The glazed walkway is an integral part of the design and the experience, allowing southbound travellers to enjoy the tower restaurant.

T P Bennett & Son (Bill Galloway and Ray Anderson), Forton Services, Lancaster, 1966. The 'Pennine Tower' dominates the scheme with its dramatic cantilevered and hard-edged geometry.

Internally the podium cafeterias and tower restaurant were built with free plans; the internal walls, being non-structural, allowed changes to be made as and when required. Even the tower gallery was designed to accommodate an additional enclosed storey should the need arise. Clearly both Rank and T.P. Bennett's team saw that the demands on the scheme would grow as the M6 itself expanded and so built in planned expansion. What they did not foresee, however, was that as traffic increased the average stop time decreased, and so the need for a waitress-service restaurant eventually disappeared. The emphasis would instead turn to self-service and thus the tower facilities would ultimately, and rather sadly, become obsolete. By 1989 they were closed to the public.

The closure of the Pennine Tower does not detract from Anderson and Galloway's extraordinary vision, which remains a landmark example of Massive-period Brutalism, exciting, avant-garde and resolutely modern.

Cumbernauld Town Centre

As has been touched on already, the concept of town planning was critical to the development of post-war architecture. This is, fairly obviously, because the regeneration of Britain following the destruction caused by a long and protracted war presented architects and planners with an almost unrivalled opportunity to make significant progress in this field. In spite of this fertile backdrop, though, the rising differences of opinion between the younger generation of architects and those of the previous generation, particularly in the Modern Movement, meant that progress was, to some, frustratingly slow. Writing in the *Architectural Review* in 1957, the architectural critic J.M. Richards commented, 'the products of ten years of rebuilding are little different to look at from what they would have been before the war'.

Although the broader scene of redevelopment in Britain and Europe was viewed by some as unexciting, there were pockets of radical and even revolutionary design during the 1950s, making the decade something of a turning point. Some of that inspiring energy could be found within the continuing programme of new towns, built following the passing of the New Towns Act 1946, and aimed at alleviating overcrowding and congestion in London and other larger British cities.

One of the cities outside London marked for new town relief was Glasgow, and one of the regions earmarked for development was Cumbernauld. Situated in North Lanarkshire only 20km (13 miles) north-east of Glasgow, the new town of Cumbernauld, designated in 1955, incorporated the existing village of the same name. A comprehensive development plan was conceived by L. Hugh Wilson, then chief architect and planning officer for the Cumbernauld Development Corporation, and involved a multi-function town centre surrounded by residential conurbations. The revolutionary concept here, though, was the complete segregation of cars and pedestrians, meaning that residents of the housing estates could access the central shops, offices and other services without ever having to cross a road. This was achieved by use of walkways, ramps and bridges, which rose above or ploughed beneath the road system.

The roadway itself was considered a masterpiece of planning at the time, anchored to the developing A80 (now M80) dual carriageway. No fewer than ten proposals were fully designed before the final plan was chosen, based on detailed and repeated traffic surveys. The expectation by 1963 was that an initial population of 20,000 would rise to 70,000 and be easily accommodated, and that provision would be made for up to 5,000 cars in the central business area.

It was the town centre scheme, though, that would become the set piece for Cumbernauld, initially celebrated but later much maligned. In 1962, Wilson was succeeded by new chief architect-planner Dudley Leaker, although Wilson was retained as a consultant. Group project architect for the centre building was Geoffrey Copcutt. The concept was to incorporate in one place everything a town would need: shops, banks, entertainment venues, restaurants, civic and commercial offices, a health centre, a post office and a small number of penthouse dwellings. The site chosen was not the easiest to work around, being on the crest of a hill, but the structure straddled this, providing pedestrian access at changing levels depending on the direction of approach.

In the December 1967 issue of *Architectural Review*, Patrick Nuttgens provides a largely complimentary critique of the town centre, likening it to 'a huge vertebrate monster'. The structure was distinctive and remains so today, bearing most, if not all, of the attributes associated with Brutalism: imposing, asymmetrical, unapologetically modern, and bristling with shuttered concrete and grey calcium silicate brickwork. It incorporated two interconnected structural systems. The first of these was developed as a concrete waffle system, which gave the ceilings the impression of coffering, while the second comprised six huge columns penetrating the main structure to support the cantilevered penthouse block.

Accessed by a road that cuts through the belly of the monster, so to speak, the lower levels provide parking and loading access to storage areas. At ground level, and accessed from pedestrian walkways or by escalator from the car parks, are shops, including a large supermarket, above which is a library and civic office with penthouse apartments above.

This phase one structure was opened by HRH Princess Margaret in 1967, by which time it had been applauded by the architectural press and profession. It had its shortcomings, though, not least of which was exposure to the sometimes harsh climate, with rain a frequent visitor and wind inadvertently 'designed' to funnel through certain areas. The grand totality of the scheme conceived in the 1950s was only partially realised, possibly because the expected population increase never materialised. The network of footpaths was confusing, the underpasses threatening and Copcutt's centre building itself, though acknowledged as the first shopping mall in the UK, topped a national poll in 2005 to decide the nation's ugliest building.

The Elephant and Castle

Before the end of the Second World War, plans were drawn up to deal with the issue of urban regeneration, particularly in those areas hardest hit by the blitz. With large areas of greater London damaged or destroyed by bombs, there came an opportunity to tackle other concerns besides the rebuilding. Sir Patrick Abercrombie's *County of London Plan* of 1943 set out to deal with poor housing, the provision of open spaces, and traffic congestion among other concerns. One of the areas under consideration by Abercrombie was the Elephant and Castle, just south of the Thames, which he foresaw as a mixture of commercial and residential spaces and structures, acting as a southerly conduit into central London. Shortly after the war ended, the then London County Council took on board Abercrombie's recommendations and began consultations on rebuilding and restructuring the district plan.

After several proposals had been sought and reviewed, that of the Hungarian-born architect Ernö Goldfinger was accepted in 1960. The hub of Goldfinger's scheme was a large, reinforced concrete block arranged as a geometric cluster of varying heights, linked by glazed walkways and arranged around an open public space. Though

solid and predominant, the blocks had a highly plastic form with seemingly random projections and recesses. These served to break up the profile of the structure so that the eye is allowed to roam the exterior surfaces and explore its contours, preventing the facades from being flat and featureless, which would have been far too cold and unrelenting in the surroundings.

The structures were composed of reinforced concrete frames with infill panels beneath the windows, the main structural framework being accentuated on the exterior, allowing form to follow function, as was Goldfinger's preference.

The first tenant of the main blocks, known as 'Site 2', was the Ministry of Health and it is from this that it gained the name Alexander Fleming House, after the discoverer of penicillin. Construction continued and Goldfinger added to the scheme with his Odeon cinema completed in 1967. This was perhaps the only truly Brutalist cinema building in Britain, with the exception of the Brunswick Centre (explored in chapter 6) and was certainly one of the most prominent commercial buildings of its day. Like the office blocks, the Odeon, although on a much smaller scale, was full of incident, the exterior articulating the interior spaces with the architect's characteristic projections and recesses.

In spite of its importance, the cinema building was demolished in the late 1980s and more recently Alexander Fleming House has been converted from offices into private apartments, its name changed to Metro Central Heights and its facades painted. The impact of the scheme is nonetheless not diminished, although the central courtyard is no longer accessible to the public. It remains, though, a key influential structure in the Massive Brutalist period.

Since the dawn of the industrial age, factory building has been an increasingly important aspect of the architectural scene. The shift from an historicist to a Modernist philosophy of building in the early twentieth century took functional buildings to a new level. Indeed, industrial buildings were at the very heart of Modernism, primarily due to their association with machines and the workings of the modern age, but also because their form was

Ernö Goldfinger, Alexander Fleming House (now Metro Central Heights), Elephant and Castle, London, 1967. The texture of this building with projections and recesses is a characteristic of the architect and appears throughout his work.

Ernö Goldfinger, Alexander Fleming House (now Metro Central Heights), Elephant and Castle, London, 1967. The main blocks are supported on square pilotis which coincide with the wall slabs, articulating the internal structure on the exterior elevations. The form of the building follows its function.

Ernö Goldfinger, Alexander Fleming House (now Metro Central Heights), Elephant and Castle, London, 1967. This section of the slab block seems to hint at later work, presaging Balfron and Trellick Towers.

largely dictated by their function. Industrial structures of the eighteenth and nineteenth centuries were often adorned with Neo-classical or Gothic-revival ornament and their proportions were rooted in the classical tradition. But the new architecture changed that, stripped away the unnecessary adornment and let the buildings be shaped by the needs of the processes that would be carried out inside them. From Peter Behrens's Turbine Factory we see spreadingww through Europe in the early twentieth century modern industrial buildings becoming part of the debate within the new

ERNÖ GOLDFINGER (1902–87)

One of the first generation of Modernist architects, Goldfinger was to have a significant impact on the post-war Brutalist period among his much younger peers in the profession. Born in Budapest, he moved with his family to Vienna in 1919 but continued his education in Switzerland and Paris where he won a scholarship to the École des Beaux-Arts to study architecture. Although benefiting from the technical training, he found the conservatism of the school stifling and turned to established architects such as Auguste Perret and Le Corbusier for guidance. In 1934 he married a British art student, Ursula Blackwell, whom he had met in Paris two years earlier, and together they moved to London. Here he joined the MARS group (Modern Architectural Research Society) and associated with radical young British architects such as Wells Coates, as well as with the influx of émigrés from Germany and Russia including Walter Gropius, Serge Chermayeff and Berthold Lubetkin. The last of these built an International Style apartment block in Hampstead, Highpoint, in which the Goldfingers rented a flat during the building work of what was to be their home for the next fifty years or so nearby at 1–3 Willow Road which Ernö had designed. The house was something of a contrast to the 'white box' aesthetic that dominated Modernist villa design in its use of exposed brick and classical proportions. It was designed to complement the early nineteenth-century dwellings around it, but, in spite of this, met with considerable, although unsuccessful, opposition.

During the war years Goldfinger worked on plans to regenerate bomb-damaged London, but his actual commissions immediately after the war seem somewhat scant. Among the most notable were an office and print works for the *Daily Worker* newspaper in Clerkenwell, London (1946), and an office for Carr & Co. in Shirley, Birmingham (1956), the latter clearly taking inspiration from Le Corbusier's *Unité d'Habitation*. At this time, significantly, Goldfinger came into contact with Alison and Peter Smithson, who found much to admire in his work and included examples of it in their 1956 exhibition 'This Is Tomorrow' at the Whitechapel Art Gallery.

In 1959 Goldfinger was given the opportunity to work on a large-scale scheme which formed part of the redevelopment of the Elephant and Castle area, the office complex first occupied by Alexander Fleming House. As the scheme took shape during the early 1960s, Goldfinger won commissions for residential housing blocks, first in Poplar and then Notting Hill. These were, respectively, the infamous Balfron and Trellick Towers, which are now celebrated and derided in equal measure. Goldfinger's place in the post-war Modernist scene was sealed and his extraordinary vision had become indelibly stamped on the landscape.

architectural sphere. Mart Stam's Van Nelle factory in Rotterdam and Owen Williams's Boots warehouse in Nottingham used large expanses of glass around steel and concrete structures, materials that were redolent of the age and heralded a new status for commercial and industrial buildings, worthy of the interest of the most progressive practitioners.

Also in Nottingham, Arup Associates were commissioned to construct the new offices and factory for the cigarette manufacturer John Player. Known as the Horizon building both during and after its construction which was completed in 1971, this low-profile box set a standard for outer-city factory units for the next two decades. It was anything but bland and unexciting, the exterior being a mixture of unadorned concrete with open cluster columns supporting a faceted frieze around the top, beneath which the white coloured and textured concrete facing was pre-cast with window apertures forming a grid. The structure accommodated a massive free-plan factory and packaging space, sandwiched between the service and plant rooms with offices on the upper and lower floors.

Richard Seiffert, Centre Point, New Oxford Street, London, 1971. The narrowness of the block is apparent end on, as are the bisected structure and the 'honeycomb' window mullions.

The project ran very smoothly throughout, Arup Associates taking the unconventional step of involving the building contractor Bovis in the design process from the outset. This was not an entirely incongruous arrangement for the practice as Arup was already an existing association of engineers and architects who combined their skills. Bringing Bovis into the field from the start was simply the next logical step in this process, the evolution of architectural practice.

Office buildings, by their nature of being located in central business districts, generally have to make the best use of restricted spaces. And it is for this reason that building upwards, as the technology progressed to make it possible, became a key characteristic of commercial architecture. But Brutalism was a style suited to megastructures which tended to be most at home in sprawling, low- or medium-rise schemes. The heavy proportions, the interplay of volumes, the asymmetrical plan and profile worked best when laid outwards rather than upwards. However, the style did become adapted to more skyward-reaching projects as has been seen at the North Wales Police Headquarters and Spence's Hyde Park Barracks. In central London, with land prices as high as they get and space at a premium, the need to build higher was ever present during the Brutalist period. One of the first of the capital's concrete commercial skyscrapers was Llewellyn Davies's Stock Exchange Building on Old Broad Street, completed in 1969 (since demolished). The heavily ribbed structure rose out of the ground like a mighty crystalline tower, almost Gothic in its perpendicular form. As in the Police HQ, it was a Brutalist version of the slab and podium arrangement, but far removed from Lever House in its vigorous muscular profile.

Centre Point

Shortly before the London Stock Exchange was completed another central London landmark was unveiled, Richard Seifert's Centre Point

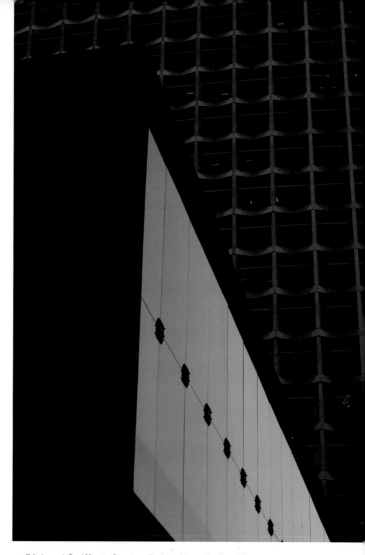

Richard Seiffert, Centre Point, New Oxford Street, London, 1971. From New Oxford Street the podium floats above the pavement on shaped columns which unify this element with the tower.

on New Oxford Street, which was completed in 1966, although it remained unoccupied for several years. The project comprised a slender, ovoid-section tower beside a wide block podium, the main tower itself at thirty-two storeys standing 117m (385ft) and providing nearly 28,000sq.m (300,000sq.ft) of floorspace. The profile of the tower is striking in its slenderness, a characteristic for which it was criticized as it restricted office space around the central core; it appears from the outside like a honeycomb sliver. The elliptical footprint was arranged in two halves, accentuated on the exterior, and the whole tower

Richard Seiffert, Centre Point, New Oxford Street, London, 1971. The tall and narrow slab block has great impact but lacked interior flexibility.

Richard Seiffert, Centre Point, New Oxford Street, London, 1971. The piano nobile with access deck raised up and projecting over the street on geometric-shaped massive columns which carry the theme from the main tower windows.

and podium were raised at first-floor level on massive geometric struts. This use of geometry was carried on in the reticulated window mullions, which are shaped with shallow V angles and seem to ripple up and down the tower's faces. Like the Smithsons' *Economist* building, Centre Point was built with a *piano nobile*, with taller window bays on the third floor, reflecting the cantilevered, curtain-glass facade of the podium on its New Oxford Street elevation, which adds a sense of stability, well needed at the base of such a narrowly proportioned structure.

On the top floor, the canopy floats on cantilevers, adding to the lightness and elegance of the scheme.

Seifert continued to add prominent London tower blocks to his portfolio, including the NatWest Tower on Old Broad Street (1981), close to the Stock Exchange building. While Centre Point was listed as Grade II in 1995, the Stock Exchange sadly did not enjoy such protection and so underwent a complete facelift in 2006, converting it into a much less adventurous glass tower.

Peter Wormersley

The Scottish architect Peter Wormersley had been commissioned to build a private house for the émigré Yugoslav textile designer Bernat Klein which was completed in 1957. High Sunderland, at Galashiels in the Scottish Borders, was a low-rise Miesian building with a rectangular plan enclosing a courtyard. With the use of large glazing areas and accentuated horizontals and verticals, the result bore strong resemblances to the sort of private villa that followed the template of Mies van der Rohe's Barcelona Pavilion (1929), such as Mies's own house at Plano, Illinois (1950) or Charles and Ray Eames's house in Santa Monica, California (1949). Two key elements, though, set High Sunderland apart from similar houses: the use of colour and the use of natural materials, namely, wood cladding, which helped the building to engage with its surroundings. Wormersley, being a friend of Klein, who admired his skills as an architect, was therefore the natural choice of designer for a new textile studio to be built on a nearby plot.

Peter Wormersley, Bernat Klein Studio, Galashiels, 1972. A 'Miesian' glass box in a woodland setting but with strong horizontal emphasis from the reinforced concrete edge beams. (Image courtesy of Roger and Jane Kelly).

With this studio, completed in 1972, Wormersley brought to bear definite Brutalist elements of the Massive convention, although one can still discern a basic Miesian framework under the skin. The two floors with roof terrace have complete, 360-degree glazing, affording exceptional views of the steeply sloping site. The first floor cantilevers out on all sides above the ground, supported by square pillars which join the heavy concrete side panels, and then this motif is repeated above with the roof terrace but supported by more slender double columns. The service

towers and interior walls are of dark blue brick, as is the ground-floor platform. At the first-floor level, there is access to and from the building by a bridge clad in concrete which extends out from the central edge beam, pushing into the wooded hillside and sited directly above the ground floor entrance.

The design, although conspicuous, nevertheless works in sympathy with the landscape, the broad areas of glass reflecting back the undulating landscape and abundant foliage around. On the inside the eye is drawn to the panoramic

Peter Wormersley, Bernat Klein Studio, Galashiels, 1972. The 360 degree glazing gives superb views while the concrete contrasts well with the blue brick service tower. (Image courtesy of Roger and Jane Kelly).

views, which give precisely the sort of even distribution of daylight that a design studio would
need. The building achieved both the RIBA and
the Edinburgh Architectural Association awards
in 1973 and has been protected by a Class A
Scottish listing. When Klein no longer used it as
a studio it eventually became a design resource
for Scottish Enterprise Borders, a regional invest-
ment agency, but it has more recently undergone
conversion into a residential property.

The Building Design Partnership

In the Massive period the characteristics of heavy
interconnecting forms, large areas of unadorned
concrete and a robustly Modernist approach
to the brief were key elements to Brutalist building. In Halifax, the Building Design Partnership

Building Design Partnership, Halifax Building Society headquarters, Halifax, 1974. An innovative office solution within a confined and awkwardly shaped space using consistent geometry throughout as well as attention to detail and high quality of finish and materials. (Image courtesy of Adam Kerfoot-Roberts).

brought these ingredients together in their scheme for the eponymous building society's headquarters on Commercial Road in central Halifax.

The site was a typically awkward one for the kind of location – a rhomboidal wedge between Commercial Road, St John's Lane to the south and Trinity Road to the north. The Building Design Partnership (BDP) filled the space by lifting the massive, glass-clad main block on four double triangular service towers, so the main bulk of the building hovers above the ground. This use of glass-clad slab supported by massive columns owes much to Owen Williams's Boots warehouse, but BDP's use of this form was dictated both by the site and the client's brief.

BDP clearly took the angular form of the site and invested the whole project with this geometry, designing the ground-floor entrance stairs, the shape of the service towers, the interior spaces, even the air-conditioning vents which took on the same rhomboidal outline as the site. Indeed, the whole building and its element parts relate back directly to the highly angular X form of the company's primary corporate identity.

The original brief called for an air-conditioned complex which would include an enclosed executive and director's suite of offices as well as wide, open-plan space for a Bürolandschaft ('office landscape') arrangement covering the whole 4,650sq.m (50,000sq.ft) area of the site. This aspect was resolved by lifting the main block up and sandwiching the Bürolandschaft between the air-conditioning plant, which also served to provide structural support, and the executive offices on the top floor.

The notion of Bürolandschaft, as the name suggests, was German in origin and developed in the 1950s and 1960s from American open-plan office arrangements, where management would interact on the same floorspace as staff to engender better and more productive communication. The use of partitions and plants subdivided the space without creating insurmountable barriers and enclosures.

Beneath the main block and arranged around the central core of lifts and stairs were the entrance hall, restaurant, store rooms and also locker rooms, with an office above. Below ground level were located the filing and other store rooms. The exterior plaza and lower structure were clad in warm yellow York stone, with the upper, two-storey block double-glazed with bronze-tinted glass set in bronze anodized aluminium frames. The effect is one of high quality in materials and a remarkable attention to detail in bringing together the required elements in a scheme that celebrates its awkwardly shaped site, reflecting the geometry from the ground up and in every corner.

One of Richard Seifert's other commercial buildings in London was less critically acclaimed, but, nevertheless, became a distinctive Brutalist landmark. The Park Tower Hotel is another adaptation of the slab and podium form, although, like Centre Point, it is far removed from its Miesian origins. Here in Knightsbridge, Seifert's tower is a rotunda with protruding window bays forming vertical ribs, giving the whole a rather knobbly organic form, like a pineapple or a hand grenade. The podium this stands on is less plastic with slightly off-set rectangular volumes in rough, pre-cast concrete with occasional windows. This aspect of the building was criticized for being less interesting and, less dynamic than the tower; and at street level the use of incident is key to engaging the public who are using the building or even just passing by. However, one could argue that too much incident at street level would have detracted from the main feature, the tower, which should command the most attention.

During the 1960s and 1970s there was a boom in tourism and visits to London were recognized as constituting an important industry that needed encouragement. The result was the Development of Tourism Act, 1969. Hotel building, therefore, increased in the capital during this time and planning legislation was relaxed to ensure that projects did not falter. In 1966 plans were set down to develop a site between Knightsbridge and Lowndes Square which contained retail and some residential buildings. The owners, Capital and Counties Property, chose

Construction involved a central service core with rooms arranged around this in groups of twenty on each of the tower's fifteen floors. On the exterior, the room windows project outwards on vertical ribs, recalling the honeycomb window mullions on Centre Point, but perhaps more so Leicester University's Attenborough Tower. This latter similarity is no coincidence as project engineers at Park Tower were Arup Associates. Though the tower is supported on pilotis, these were buried within the two-storey podium structure which contained the reception area, bars and restaurant.

More recently, the Knightsbridge elevation at street level has been adapted with retail and leisure spaces, although they do nothing to enhance the podium, which would have looked better unmolested. Here, like Centre Point, we see Brutalism standing almost in spite of the surrounding buildings, although its scale remains at least sympathetic. This, though, was Modernism daring to stand out and be noticed.

Richard Seiffert, Park Tower Hotel (now Sheraton Park Tower), Knightsbridge, London, 1973. The stylish and dynamic tower rests on a less successful podium, the whole bristling with texture typical of the architect and project engineers Arup Associates.

Richard Seifert & Partners, but the initial design was rejected by the LCC as being too much at odds with the existing buildings around it. A new design with a 55m (180ft) tower was proposed and, once approved, the project went ahead, reaching completion in 1973. It is interesting to note that Seifert's hotel was built within eyeshot of Basil Spence's Hyde Park Barracks, with its tower standing nearly 40m (130ft) taller. When it opened the building was occupied by the Canadian Skyline company and its first operational name was the Skyline Park Tower Hotel.

St Giles Hotel

Also experiencing the more relaxed planning rules in London following the passing of the Development of Tourism Act was Elsworth Sykes Partnership's St Giles Hotel and YMCA, completed in 1977. The site on Bedford Avenue was that of the former YMCA, an impressive Edwardian building, which was demolished in 1971 to make way for a new structure. Much like the Sheraton Tower, this was a design of two distinct zones. At street level the appearance is somewhat unexciting, with shop frontages on the Tottenham Court Road elevation beneath bands of ribbon windows set within textured concrete facing panels. This forms the podium upon which four slab towers rest. It is in these towers that the design becomes more visually commanding. Each thrusts upwards, the surface bristling with rhythmic texture in the form of vertical bands of narrow windows set within deep concrete mullions and arranged at angles to form a sawtooth

ABOVE: Elsworth Sykes Partnership, St.Giles Hotel and YMCA, Bedford Avenue, London, 1977. The cluster of towers rise above the pavement on massive concrete cantilevers, integrating well with the ground-floor facades.

OPPOSITE: Elsworth Sykes Partnership, St.Giles Hotel and YMCA, Bedford Avenue, London, 1977. The towers were designed at different heights and spaced apart, the windows set into sawtooth projections, all designed to allow natural light in as well as views out from all of the rooms.

arrangement reminiscent of Spence's Coventry Cathedral. The towers are clustered together and interconnected at the centre, the 670 guest rooms arranged in units of six, seven, nine and twelve storeys. The surfaces project and recess on each elevation to allow each room a view of the street and the towers float above the podium on heavy beams, which allow them to cantilever outwards over the pavements below.

The overall effect is more successful than Seifert's hotel at Knightsbridge, where the synthesis between the podium and the tower seems less convincing. St Giles Hotel is unapologetically modern amid much older historicist buildings. Its vigorous and dynamic exterior does, nevertheless, reflect the internal structure and the needs of the brief to allow natural light to reach all the rooms.

The City of London district has evolved over the last 200 years to become one of the most diverse built environments in the country and it continues to change all the time. Since the construction of Sir John Soane's Bank of England on Threadneedle Street (1788–1833), the area has contained some of the most stylish and innovative architecture built in Britain. In spite of the many great contrasts in this small part of London, there is nothing jarring or out of place. Perhaps because of the industry based here, international finance, the quality of materials and design has had a unifying effect on these diverse buildings. Perhaps also the centuries of trade and commerce that have shaped and informed the area have resulted in a resilience and a creativity that can accommodate massive change.

Salters' Livery Company

When the Salters' Livery Company headquarters in Bread Street burned down in 1941 a replacement design was sought, although the process was a protracted one lasting into the 1970s.

One of the most progressive partnerships was commissioned to take on the work, Spence Bonnington and Collins. At the time, they were in the process of building Kensington and Chelsea Town Hall and so came highly recommended. The chosen site on Fore Street was somewhat constrained, integrating with the Barbican high walk on one side and St Alphage Gardens on the other. The finished building rose up above the street like a ship, with its distinctive, cantilevered stair chamber and the exterior clad in white concrete, which was textured with ribs or brush hammering to create a very tactile and high quality finish.

The original brief called for a multiple-use space, including the company's administrative offices, a livery hall for banqueting and other entertainment and also a range of offices available for lease. In order to provide all this on such a restricted footprint, the livery hall was cantilevered out on all sides, accessed by a stair-case which was also cantilevered out over the high walkway, thereby saving considerable internal space.

The structure was concrete framed with over 800 tonnes (785 tons) of reinforcing steel, containing in situ slab floors, 24cm (9.5in) thick in the office section and 90cm (35.4in) thick in the livery hall. Two of the principal features of the building were the quality of the materials and the finish. The exposed concrete was mixed with Hopton Wood aggregate to provide a white finish, much of which was textured in various patterns. The over-sailing stair tower was coffered on the underside, and on the St Alphage Gardens elevation the office spaces below the cantilevered hall were expressed with tinted glass within bronzed aluminium vertical mullions.

Salters' Hall has withstood the test of time well, although the exterior walls have been painted to retain their whiteness. It has continued to be used for its original purpose well into the twenty-first century and sits happily within the quiet environs of the City and the Barbican complex. Indeed, it is best viewed from the Barbican elevated walkway, where the full impact can be enjoyed that is almost impossible to see from ground level on Fore Street. Alternatively, when viewed from the secluded St Alphage Gardens one can digest the quality of the materials and the design rising above the ancient wall.

OPPOSITE: *John S Bonnington Partnership (Basil Spence), Salters' Hall, City of London, 1976. A Massive Period feast of clashing concrete volumes appearing like a stylized ship from the raised walkways.*

LEFT: *John S Bonnington Partnership (Basil Spence), Salters' Hall, City of London, 1976, cantilevered stair tower showing high attention to detail and quality of materials, the concrete cladding coloured white and textured.*

John S Bonnington Partnership (Basil Spence), Salters' Hall, City of London, 1976, the St Alphage Garden elevation showing surface texture, incident and interplay of light in a confined space.

While the Miesian glass and steel aesthetic served the commercial world well in the post-war years, it was a framework that followed more or less the same template whether in London, Manchester, New York or Chicago. Brutalism, on the other hand, seemed to find a multitude of guises; the style seemed adaptable to all manner of briefs and sites, both constrained and open. Brutalism was free from the strictures of symmetry and so could be moulded to suit the needs of the client as well as of the site, no matter how awkward. Brutalism was also adaptable stylistically and architects could apply a range of finishes and materials to exterior and interior surfaces which seem to contradict the dour and heavy reputation that the style had earned for itself. Commercial briefs undoubtedly provided more flexible budgets and solutions varied widely, asking a little more of Brutalism in this sector, stretching it to new heights, quite literally, and forcing it to look ahead a little further and adopt some longevity. In the commercial world Brutalism became stylish as well as functional, being required to act as a living advertisement for its occupiers as well as an efficient place of work.

OTHER NOTABLE BRUTALIST COMMERCIAL BUILDINGS

Penguin Books Warehouse, Harmondsworth, Middlesex (Arup Associates, 1973): a lesson in making warehouse architecture interesting, with narrow concrete fin columns supporting V-shaped roof troughs with full-length ceiling lights. The exterior clad in brick between the columns, breaking up the surface and adding texture.

Tricorn Centre, Portsmouth (now demolished) (Owen Luder and Rodney Gordon, 1966): achieving iconic Brutalist status due to its stark unbridled concrete and interplay of volumes, reviled by many, like Cumbernauld, as representing the worst face of brutal Modernism.

Denys Lasdun and Partners, IBM Offices, South Bank, London, 1978–84. The West elevation facing the National Gallery showing the softening use of brick and the recessed entrance front beneath heavily overhanging upper storeys showing influences from Frank Lloyd Wright.

continued overleaf

OTHER NOTABLE BRUTALIST COMMERCIAL BUILDINGS continued

IBM Headquarters, South Bank, London (Denys Lasdun, 1984): like its neighbouring National Theatre there is much horizontal banding and 'strata' with both concrete and brick cladding as well as large expanses of glass. The concrete facing panels mixed with a dense aggregate left rough-textured, the handrails harking back to International Style aesthetics.

Denys Lasdun and Partners, IBM Offices, South Bank, London, 1978–84. On the North elevation facing The Thames there is an interplay of volumes and strong International Style imagery in the ribbon windows and hand rails.

Chapter 5

Building for Leisure and Entertainment

The concept of leisure for the masses is one that was established during the nineteenth century when the development of steam and a network of railways brought coastal resorts and other places of interest within the reach of the many instead of the fortunate few. In the early twentieth century leisure time was seen as an essential counterpoint to the drudgery of work for the larger proportion of the nation and was encouraged as a means of keeping workforces contented. This provided a source of important commissions for architects and occasionally gave opportunities to demonstrate the flexibility of Modernism in this field. During the 1930s examples such as Mendelsohn and Chermayeff's De La Warr Pavillion and Lubetkin and Tecton's Regent's Park Zoo penguin pool were at the leading edge and brought Modernism into the wider public domain.

The restructuring and rebuilding of towns and cities after the war meant that further opportunities existed for the second generation of Modernists who had been looking to Le Corbusier and following his post-war lead with béton brut megastructures. Celebrated or infamous projects such as the Tricorn Centre at Portsmouth by Rodney Gorden and the Owen Luder Partnership (1966; demolished) and Geoffrey Copcutt's Cumbernauld town centre and shopping precinct (1968) seemed at the time to answer all the needs of a modern society that was increasingly dependent on the motor car. In this sector there is a mix of commissions between the commercial and the civic and certainly the financial clout of commercial developers helped to get some projects off the ground faster and benefited, like the Tricorn Centre and Cumbernauld, from planning authorities who resisted the reactionary objections to Modernism and opened the way for such projects to be given life.

The Chichester Festival Theatre

Completed in 1961, this was a bold new departure from conventional 'proscenium arch' designs and captured the new mood in theatrical performance pioneered by the likes of John Osborne, Alan Ayckbourn and Lawrence Olivier. It was also a pioneering architectural statement and heralded the coming of the Massive phase in Brutalism. Built by Powell and Moya, the structure adopted a rather Behrensian nature; the exterior shape dictated by the interior spaces – form following function. The interior comprised a projecting, five-sided stage with steeply raked seating for 1,360 arranged around it. The exterior was octagonal in form, the seating cantilevered out and up on cranked columns. This created a distinctive profile, almost mushroom-like from certain angles and presaging Bennett's Pennine Tower at Lancaster Service Station, which seems to grow out of the ground in its parkland setting.

The building was constructed using primarily in situ concrete, the upper part with auditorium seating and stage raised on six reinforced, concrete columns, those at the entrance front set back and projecting up and out to support the cantilevered upper floor. This forms a dramatic canopy over the entrance foyer and accentuates the overall geometry of the building. Beyond the foyer on the ground floor, space remained for cloakrooms, offices and dressing rooms beneath the stage. The decision to design the space as an octagon was based on reducing costs, but also on acoustics which were deemed to be superior to those of a circular auditorium.

At the outer edge of the cantilevers a reinforced concrete ring beam runs around the circumference at gallery level, tying the cantilever columns to counteract the stresses on the front section. The front three beams continue upwards vertically at this point and form part of the roof support. The roof itself is a tent-like, steel canopy, anchored with cables and tied into the corners of the building. To counteract the downward forces of the cantilevered upper auditorium, the side walls of the building contained buttresses to anchor the structure to its site.

The arrangement of the interior is where innovation in theatre design becomes more pronounced. The architects consulted Sir Tyrone Guthrie and Sir Lawrence (later Lord) Olivier and developed a space specifically for the emerging trend in performance, which moved towards a more direct, almost interactive, engagement between the actors and the audience. The stage was designed to appear bare with no scenery or set design to distract the audience from the performance itself, a balcony stage and plain wooden screen being virtually the only tools available to the actors and directors, along with lighting rigs set into the exposed ceiling.

The overall design was one of simplicity to reflect the stripped stage, but was nonetheless dramatic and full of impact. The exterior concrete was left grey with infilling wall panels on the upper level painted dark brown, while on the ground floor the vertical strip window mullions were painted white, as was the wood strip cladding on the two glazed stairwells. These uses of colour and texture were designed to echo the flint, brick and whitewash of Chichester's vernacular buildings. Remarkably the structure was completed in a year and yet was of such quality in design and materials that it has remained in constant use since its opening.

OPPOSITE ABOVE: Powell & Moya,
Chichester Festival Theatre, 1961. The rear elevation
with enclosed stair tower behind its painted wood
slatting, the side walls buttressed to counteract
tipping forces at the front.

OPPOSITE BELOW: Powell & Moya,
Chichester Festival Theatre, 1961. Front elevation
showing its parkland setting and the 'mushroom'
shape of the auditorium projecting outwards over the
entrance foyer.

The London South Bank

The South Bank in London had acted as the platform for a post-war tonic, a celebration of British achievement and a glance at what the future might hold, wrapped up in the great public exhibition that was the Festival of Britain. What remained after the Festival had closed and the site was cleared was one of the most important civic buildings of the era – Leslie Martin's Royal Festival Hall. The question then remained of how to do justice to this legacy and develop the site in a constructive way. The incoming Conservative government saw the Festival as a Socialist legacy that needed to be cleared away, but in 1964 Labour returned to power and so cultural projects on the site gained more impetus. The LCC by then had already begun to extend the Festival Hall with additional auditoria and the site to the east of this up to Waterloo Bridge,

Denys Lasdun and Partners, The National Theatre, London, 1976. North riverfront elevation showing the strong horizontal forms and interlocking volumes.

where, during the Festival, the Centenary Pavilion and Harbour Bar were arranged around the Lambeth shot tower, was earmarked for a mixed-use arts centre. The architect who had carried out the additional work to the Hall, Hubert Bennett, led the team to build two music auditoria and an art gallery.

Completed in 1967–68, the Queen Elizabeth Hall, the Purcell Room and the Hayward Gallery were together a masterclass in Massive Brutalist concrete. The forms were highly geometric and were brought together in an asymmetric cluster, with cantilevered volumes projecting out over the raised walkways. To some extent, the elevations enunciated the spaces within, but the collection of blank, textured, concrete faces reveals little more and the whole project took on the monumental ambiguity typical of Massive-period Brutalism. The

structure was composed of in situ wall and floor beams with a mixture of exposed elements, patterned with their timber shuttering and pre-cast cladding panels textured with aggregate.

In 1949 the hundred-year campaign to establish a national theatre company came to a happy conclusion with the passing of the National Theatre Bill and so a new theatre building was needed to house it. The South Bank Board was charged with the task, working in conjunction with the Shakespeare Memorial National Theatre Committee. After several proposals for the location were explored, a site was chosen in 1967 which was to the west of Waterloo Bridge, adjacent to the South Bank Centre, which was still under construction. Denys Lasdun had been one of twenty shortlisted architects to be interviewed by the committee and impressed the members with his passion for the project, his deep personal involvement and, curiously, his lack of experience. Having never designed a theatre, he brought a freshness, an eye without preconceptions and a desire to learn from the committee all he needed to know about the work to be done.

Originally the intention was also to include a National Opera House within the theatre complex, but restricted funding and the shape of the site settled on both precluded this. What emerged from Lasdun's consultation with the committee, though, was the need to have more than one theatre space to accommodate the several functions of the building. This allowed for the creation of three distinct theatre types: classical Greek, proscenium arch and Tudor courtyard. Construction began in 1967 and the theatre was opened in stages as the spaces were completed, the first in 1976.

Denys Lasdun and Partners, The National Theatre, London, 1976. The use of light and form is dramatic, the concrete left unpolished with its shuttering clearly visible, a theme continued on the interior.

Denys Lasdun and Partners, The National Theatre, London, 1976. At the riverside entrance the stair tower has off-set geometry and intersects the cantilevered floors like a crystalline structure.

The location on a sharp bend in the River Thames, with Waterloo Bridge to one side, brought a clear triangular geometry to the scheme which is reflected throughout the building, lending a certain Expressionist, crystalline quality to it. He carried through the concept of 'strata' from his East Anglia University project and applied it here, with the layered walkways and terraced access galleries providing a strong horizontal emphasis as well as reducing the monumentality of the building. These strata are intersected by the off-set angled stair towers which penetrate through the floors and project upwards over the main roof line. Dominating the same roof line are the two fly towers. These structures were designed to contain the machinery used to move scenery up and down above the stages and are contained in two cuboid blocks, so redolent of Lasdun. These are graded in height, again to counteract the largeness of scale and, on the river elevation, to unify the structural elements into a strong triangular form.

The structure was largely composed of in situ floor and wall beams with some pre-cast elements, predominantly finished with the wood-slat moulding lines, unpolished but yet carefully applied to form surface patterns. This theme continued on the larger interior spaces and, although considered by some to be too stark and industrial, the finish was of such high quality that it was able to make a strong statement and stand the test of time.

Chamberlin, Powell and Bon, The Barbican Centre, London, 1952-82. The circle and towers showing a mixture of scale, materials and finishes.

The Barbican

One of the largest building schemes of the post-war period was for a site of around 18ha (45 acres) in the Cripplegate area of central London, close to the City and the financial district, which had suffered considerable bomb damage. It was a site of historical significance, containing fragments of the second-century Roman wall. Intersected by Beech Street, the development brief covered two main areas: that to the north around Golden Lane and that to the south which became known as the Barbican (after the Latin *barbecana*, meaning a fortified gateway or outpost). The City of London Corporation held an open competition for the project in 1951; this was won by the Kingston School of Architecture teacher Geoffrey Powell, who teamed with two colleagues from the School, Christof Bon and Peter Chamberlin. For the next thirty years they would work together on the project, which would contain a high-density housing scheme, arts complex, schools and shops within its protective walls.

The project was tackled in stages, starting with the housing estate at Golden Lane, but nonetheless unfolded into a cohesive whole. The unity of the design is most clearly seen, though, on the Barbican site, where the principles of Le Corbusier, with a mixture of different functionalities, could be combined in one discrete area, providing for all the needs of a community. But there was a wider remit than simply providing for the residents of the scheme, although this was of paramount importance. The Barbican Arts Centre would also act as a leisure and conference attraction to bring people in from all over the capital and much further afield.

This was the last phase of the development constructed between 1971 and 1982 and comprised a crescent-shaped complex containing a theatre, a concert hall, an art gallery, a restaurant, shops and a public library, as well as a music school, youth hostel, swimming pool and gym, in addition to housing for around 6,500 more people. At the heart of the complex within the embrace of the crescent, a tiled plaza was created with an artificial lake and fountains providing a 'street' from which to access certain parts of the complex as well as for outside tables serving the restaurant. Here the tiled paving and the introduction of water features and planting provided needed relief from the large expanses of concrete, heavy Brutalist volumes and massive towers.

Above this level are access galleries and walkways in a seemingly bewildering arrangement, but which, nevertheless, manage to maintain a human scale and diffuse what might have been a rather threatening and oppressive environment in another location. Indeed, the quiet tranquillity of the Barbican Centre was a remarkable achievement, given the brutal nature of the aesthetics employed. This was managed by creating a cloistered environment, protected from the clamour and haste of the City, but also by maintaining a strong cultural and intellectual heart, carefully mixed and balanced with the residential areas.

OPPOSITE: Chamberlin, Powell and Bon, The Barbican Centre, London, 1952–82. On the upper level the residential areas blend seamlessly with the arts venues, carrying common motifs and materials through both parts.

BELOW: Chamberlin, Powell and Bon, The Barbican Centre, London, 1952–82. The plaza with restaurants and access to the circle hall and, on the upper levels, the art gallery, library and cinemas.

OPPOSITE ABOVE: Chamberlin, Powell and Bon, The Barbican Centre, London, 1952–82. Looking at the plaza the mix of materials is apparent including textured aggregate in situ concrete, ceramic tile and brick.

OPPOSITE FAR LEFT: Chamberlin, Powell and Bon, The Barbican Centre, London, 1952–82. The residential towers borrow motifs from the arts complex and repeat them to dramatic effect.

OPPOSITE LEFT: Chamberlin, Powell and Bon, The Barbican Centre, London, 1952–82. Beside the plaza the use of water and planting softens the impact of the heavy massing of concrete, the residential blocks here raised on a forest of pilotis.

ABOVE LEFT: Hubert Bennett, South Bank Arts Centre, London, 1967–68. Here the use of concrete and chunky forms is pure Massive Brutalism and designed for visual impact.

ABOVE RIGHT: Hubert Bennett, South Bank Arts Centre, London, 1967–68. Like Lasdun's later neighbouring National Theatre the shuttering on the exterior walls is left exposed and unpolished.

RIGHT: Hubert Bennett, South Bank Arts Centre, London, 1967–68. On the south side we see a mixture of finishes coming together; rough shuttered in situ, pre-cast polished with aggregate and textured aggregate facing panels.

Like commercial building, the remit for leisure and entertainment in the post-war period was for modernity. This meant that the commissioned architects could express the spirit of the day with challenging and exciting buildings that would invite debate but which would also have to attract people to enter them and withstand the demands made upon them on a long-term basis. Some achieved this extremely well, such as Lasdun's National Theatre. Others did not, such as its neighbour the South Bank Arts Complex, and required time and a great deal of help to get them to work at an optimum level. But like all architecture, buildings for leisure would stand up to scrutiny and continued wear and tear only if the design had been well thought out and the materials used were of the highest quality.

OTHER NOTABLE BRUTALIST BUILDINGS FOR LEISURE

Nottingham Playhouse, Nottingham (Peter Moro Partnership, 1963): a drum-shaped auditorium set within a low-rise podium, containing a traditional proscenium stage, but in a dramatic modern building.

Peter Moro Partnership, Nottingham Playhouse, Wellington Circus, Nottingham, 1963. *The drum shape of the auditorium contains a proscenium stage set within a low oblong box with its distinctive strip windows.* (Image courtesy of Iqbal Alaam)

Chapter 6

Social and Private Housing

One of the most emotive and often divisive issues of the modern age has been that of housing. During the twentieth century in Britain the key demands that faced successive governments, town planners and architects alike have been the rebuilding after war, meeting the needs of a growing population and keeping in step with the rapidly changing social, cultural and recreational needs of the nation. These were, and remain, tough and exacting circumstances to deal with successfully in a medium that is, by its very nature, static and enduring. Little wonder then that the shape of domestic architecture in Britain has seen so many changes in the last hundred years.

The quest for the ideal housing type is one that the Modernists wrestled with from the outset, but it was in designing dwellings primarily that the Modernists found the most accessible form with which to test their theories, aesthetics and structural integrity. For it was the private villa that many of the fathers of Modernism found they were most readily commissioned to build and so, throughout the first period between 1900 and 1939, a great many such houses were built in France, Germany, Holland and Britain which allowed the architects to express their ideals and discover whether and how they worked. For some, like Le Corbusier, housing was an integral part of their vision for developing urban spaces, and higher-density social housing was a utopian goal to which they aspired, planned for and theorized about. In its

early stages, Le Corbusier's vision was realized in his building for the 1925 Paris Exposition Internationale des Artes Décoratif et Industriels, the Pavillon de l'Esprit Nouveau. This small building was the embodiment of a design he referred to as the 'Immeubles Villa' or 'luxury apartment', which was designed to be a mass-produced and infinitely repeatable housing unit that could be slotted together to form large blocks of communities.

The Influence of Le Corbusier

Le Corbusier's ideas were far ahead of their time as they broached the issue of urban 'grain'. This concept, which was debated in the post-war period in relation to town planning and mass housing, suggested that the 'grain' or density of functions within a built landscape had a direct impact on the efficiency with which these spaces were used. A fine grain indicated a good blend of domestic, recreational, civic and commercial building, meaning shorter travelling distances and a much greater use of the local structures and amenities by the communities living there. A city with a broader grain would have a much greater separation of these building types, meaning long commuting distances and a poorer use of civic and recreational facilities. Le Corbusier felt that the architect had a duty to provide an environment that was spiritually fulfilling, creating harmony between people and their surroundings and freeing communities from the misery of poor housing.

In the immediate post-war period Le Corbusier finally had the opportunity to make real his utopian vision for collective housing when he was commissioned to build a block of flats in Marseille as part of a programme of public housing designed to deal with the severe shortage at the time. The Unité d'Habitation, as it was called, was designed to contain 330 apartments which were of no fewer than twenty-three different varieties, in addition to a hotel and a shopping 'street'. Here Le Corbusier was able to test his work of over two decades on dwelling design, construction techniques and town planning. It was also an opportunity to see how a community would interact in a contained, mixed-use environment. The building was completed in 1952 and set a benchmark for Modernist architects throughout the world to aspire to – not just in terms of tackling housing issues but also stylistically, as the Unité d'Habitation was an extraordinary building, encapsulating the new Brutalist aesthetic emerging in Europe with its monumental scale and rough-cast, concrete or béton brut finish.

Team 10

Team 10, or Team X, was a loose association of architects, informally established between 1953 and 1959. The roots of the team go back to 1951, when Alison and Peter Smithson attended their first meeting of the Congrès Internationaux d'Architecture Moderne (CIAM) at Hoddesdon in Hertfordshire. The CIAM had been established in 1928 by Le Corbusier and Sigfried Giedion as an international platform for modern architecture and its practitioners. It was at Hoddesden, during the eighth congress, that the Smithsons

heard Le Corbusier talk and met architects of their own generation, including Georges Candilis and Shadrach Woods.

In 1953, at the ninth CIAM congress in Aix-en-Provence, the younger generation of architects who would become Team 10 were nearly all present. Perhaps for the first time, they came into contact with one another, finding common ground and a common approach to their craft that deviated from the principles of the old guard. The CIAM could see a need to keep the organisation fresh with the influx of younger architects, and so to address this, the regional branches of the congress created special 'younger' sections that took on active roles. The result, however, was a growing schism between the younger generation of architects and their predecessors, whose views on urbanism were significantly different. The continuing debate led to a shift in the running of the organisation from older to younger generations, but the divide between the two was eventually to prove irreparable.

The group tasked with organising the CIAM conference at Dubrovnik in 1956 was dubbed 'Team 10' as the congress was the tenth to be held. The core members were Peter Smithson (representing the United Kingdom), along with Jaap Bakema (the Netherlands), Georges Candilis (France) and Rolf Gutmann (Switzerland). Le Corbusier and Walter Gropius were both absent from the meeting, although the former submitted a letter suggesting how the roles of the founders of the CIAM in 1928 and the new under-40 generation might be delineated. From this point, the official transition of the management of CIAM took place until 1959, when the last congress was held at Otterlo in the Netherlands. It was here, at Henry van de Velde's Kröller-Müller Museum, that the decision was made to effectively disband the CIAM, and so Team 10 became the new order.

Free from the bureaucratic shackles of the CIAM, Team 10 established its own platform for the debate and discussion of modern architecture, and for the solutions it presented for domestic, civic and commercial building. In the 'Team 10 Primer', a document originally written

Cover of the Team 10 Primer, *1968 edition, edited by Alison Smithson.*

by Alison Smithson for discussion at the 1961 meeting and published a year later in *Architectural Design*, the aims of the group were stated as 'concerned with inducing, as it were, into the bloodstream of the architect an understanding and feeling for the patterns, the aspirations, the artefacts, the tools, the modes of transportation and communications of present-day society, so that he can as a natural thing build towards that society's realization-of-itself'. To this end, Team 10 aimed to invent a 'working-together-technique'. The goal was to arrive at 'meaningful groupings of buildings, where each building is a live thing and a natural extension of the others. Together they will make places where a man can realize what he wishes to be.'

From 1960 until 1981, Team 10 continued to meet, discussing issues raised by the CIAM as well as tackling the broad task of post-war rebuilding and regeneration. The 1960s in particular was a time of intense activity, with many competitions established for schemes of mass housing, new universities, civic offices and so forth on a scale not seen before. The 1970s saw Team 10 retreat into a smaller core group with occasional outsiders invited in. They met in less formal circumstances but continued to debate the issues of housing and urban development. The death in 1981 of Jaap Bakema, who had been a strong driving force within the group from its beginnings and its 'coordinator', marked an effective end to the cohesion of Team 10, and no further meetings were held.

Britain between the Wars

In Britain the inter-war period had seen some experimentation in private and public housing, with varying degrees of success. There were several good villas by both indigenous and émigré architects as well as several collective housing projects both private and social. One of the earliest of these was the Isokon Group's Lawn Road Flats in Hampstead, completed in 1934 and designed by Wells Coates, and, while the rents were such that the block was clearly aimed at middle-class tenants, the realization of new concepts in minimal living spaces paved the way for more socially inspired projects. One of the more celebrated of these was E. Maxwell Fry's Kensal House in Ladbroke Grove, completed in 1937.

Commissioned by the Gas Light & Coke Company, this scheme was designed to rehouse families from cleared slum areas, an objective laid out in the Greenwood Act of 1930. What Fry and his co-designer Elizabeth Denby set out to achieve was a standard of living with community facilities hitherto unavailable to the working classes at a minimal cost. Although the two blocks built provided only sixty-eight apartments, it was a highly successful scheme and acted as a template for future slum clearances.

More or less exactly contemporary with Kensal House was one of the most iconic Modernist blocks of flats in Britain, Berthold Lubetkin and Tecton's Highpoint 1, merely a walk away from the Lawn Road flats in Hampstead. Unlike Coates's building, this one was intended to house factory workers; although more spaciously appointed, in reality this was never

Tecton (Denys Lasdun), Hallfield Estate, Paddington, London, 1948–55. The slab blocks were arranged in six and ten storeys at right angles to allow good transmission of light and maintain privacy as well as community.

Tecton (Denys Lasdun), Hallfield Estate, Paddington, London, 1948–55. The smooth tiled decks give depth and a playful geometry to the front elevations of the ten-storey blocks.

fully realized and the flats were largely occupied by the well-to-do of north London. This was the International Style in all its white stuccoed concrete glory, with oodles of ocean-liner detail, cantilevered balconies, ribbon windows, pilotis, ramped walkways and sculptural plastic forms. But it was also designed to provide a high quality of life in large apartments arranged in a cross of Lorraine form so that partition walls between the dwellings were kept to an absolute minimum, reducing noise and increasing privacy.

Tecton and After

The practice that built it, Tecton, had been formed in 1932 by Lubetkin and it was a firm that lasted into the post-war period. In 1947 Tecton were commissioned by the borough of Paddington to develop a site at Bishop's Bridge Road. The project architects were Denys Lasdun and Lindsay Drake, who, after Tecton dissolved in 1948, saw the scheme through to completion in 1955.

The brief was to provide housing for workers in light industry and to incorporate amenities such as shops, garages, laundry, schools and recreation. The borough was undergoing redevelopment as part of the London plan, moving residents from what was regarded as obsolete housing that had been earmarked for demolition since before the war. The plan was also designed to address the population explosion in the area. An article in the March 1955 issue of the Architects' Journal on the scheme cited a rise in population from 2,000 in the nineteenth century to over 138,000 then and so the need for good, high-density accommodation was acute. The aim was to house 200 people per acre and Lasdun and Drake's completed estate managed to get comfortably close to this at 176.

The estate was planned on a diagonal north–south grid, from Bishop's Bridge Road with fourteen blocks, six with ten storeys and the remaining eight with six, containing altogether 656 flats intended to provide accommodation for 2,362 people. Arranged at right angles to each other and creating informal squares and courtyards, the blocks themselves had a restrained geometry to them, clearly influenced still by the International Style and also, particularly with the six-storey blocks, a definite Lubetkin quality to them which seems to echo Highpoint II. They were constructed with reinforced concrete floor slabs, cross walls and mullions, faced in dark red- or 'dun'-coloured brick, with contrasting cream tiling and grey and white concrete facings on the access galleries.

Tecton (Denys Lasdun), Hallfield Estate, Paddington, London, 1948–55. On the six-storey blocks a similar arrangement of tiled decks articulate the inner structure and show influences from Tecton's earlier work at Highpoint II in Hampstead.

Both ten- and six-storey blocks were cantilevered out at first-floor level, with ground-floor flats recessed, supported at each end by pilotis or tapering, rough, concrete pillars, these last details being highly evocative of the Unité d'Habitation.

The galleries, accessed either by stair or lift, were faced with pre-cast panels which were contained within the end tile facings and so appeared to float on the front elevations. The design of the facings formed key patterns in varying widths, the narrower protruding out further to accent changes in depth on the galleries. Lasdun and Drake designed the flats so that none of the habitable rooms faced on to the galleries, to maintain privacy. On the six-storey blocks the galleries were marked with narrower facing

accents, while on the living room facades a series of curiously curved, shaped, private balconies project on alternate floors, to avoid overshadowing, giving these shorter blocks a sculptural quality that provides a welcome interest on these broad slabs.

The design was celebrated in its day, worked successfully as an almost complete community project and remains well maintained and highly regarded by its current residents. The fact that little has changed on the estate in the last fifty years and that there seem to be only negligible signs of age bears testament to the quality of the architecture, the layout, the provision of services and amenities and the attention to detail, all of which became Lasdun trademarks.

Tecton (Denys Lasdun), Hallfield Estate, Paddington, London, 1948–55. The rear elevation balconies are angular in shape and arranged on every other floor, breaking up the otherwise plain brick surface.

Tecton (Denys Lasdun), Hallfield Estate, Paddington, London, 1948–55. The ten-storey blocks are raised on tapering columns, showing parallels with Le Corbusier's Unité which was being built at the same time.

Denys Lasdun, Sulkin House cluster block, Bethnal Green, London, 1952. An early foray into the alternative to slab or point blocks, providing privacy for each apartment as well as noise insulation.

The Cluster Block

Even while the Hallfield estate was being built, we see a move from Early Brutalism towards the Massive style in other housing projects that Lasdun was commissioned to design in London. But the architect's careful consideration of the pre-existing landscape and buildings was to crystallize into an entirely different approach to the Corbusian slab blocks found at Hallfield. In his projects for Bethnal Green, Lasdun studied the mix and distribution of building types in the area and used this to inform the design of two important blocks, Sulkin House at Usk Street completed in 1955 and Keeling House on Clare-dale Street completed in 1958. Here we see the birth of the 'cluster' tower, essentially a grouping of two or more blocks arranged around and connected to a central service unit.

The Usk Street development was built very much on a human scale, with two boomerang-shaped towers angled slightly and standing on either side of a stair and service tower. Each apartment was of maisonette type, reflected on the exterior, which directly related to the surrounding buildings and rooted it in its environment. From a Brutalist perspective, the block has a more solid feel than Hallfield, with the towers plunging direct into the ground rather than seeming to float above it. The building was largely faced in smooth, pre-cast concrete panels, with the front and the rear living elevation slightly recessed and faced in dark grey brick with the floor and crosswall slabs projecting out, flush with the gable ends, accentuating each floor division. To the entrance front, facing Roman Road, each dwelling has its own access deck linked to the central tower with a short bridge.

Deny Lasdun, Keeling House cluster block, Bethnal Green, London, 1958. Stylistically more successful than Sulkin House and showing Lasdun's interest in horizontal banding or 'strata' and a mix of materials and textures.

On the living room sides the upper floor of each maisonette has a small balcony which projects only slightly from the gable end facings. The service tower has a rounded front facing Knottisford Street, with a narrow vertical strip window up its entire height and surmounted with a cuboid engine room, something that was to become a Lasdun trademark.

The concept of the cluster block allowed, first, for the elimination of partition walls between dwellings, perhaps inspired by Lubetkin's Highpoint I, and the separation of the stair and service tower reduced noise pollution for the interior spaces, as did placing the living rooms on the opposite side facing outwards. What this arrangement also did was to provide views through the building to the spaces and architecture beyond, further assisting the integration of the block into its surroundings.

The later building, Keeling House, on Claredale Street had four blocks arranged at a slight angle to each other around the central staircase, lift and service core. It was designed as part of a development with two six-storey blocks on a site containing bomb-damaged terraces, but intended to integrate with the surrounding, undamaged, Victorian dwellings. The cluster block would hold fifty-six maisonettes and eight bed sitting-room flats, with, as at Sulkin House, a central service core connected to the dwelling towers by bridges. The scale of the fourteen floors was purposely designed to reflect the two-storey brick terraces around it, essentially like a row of houses tipped up on its end. The arrangement of the blocks around the core allowed direct sunlight to reach all the habitable rooms and also separated access, refuse chutes and clothes-drying areas from the living rooms to increase privacy. To aid this further, the ground floor was reserved for electrical plant and heating as well as storage for bicycles, raising the living quarters to first-floor level to avoid those tenants being overlooked by people entering and leaving the building. Also, as in the blocks at Hallfield and Sulkin House, the rooms facing the access galleries were entrance halls, bathrooms, cloakrooms and internal stairs, and here at Keeling House it was possible for no fewer than 75 per cent of the tenants to reach their front door without passing any other dwellings.

The structure was essentially reinforced concrete floor slabs and gable ends, each dwelling with a single cross-wall and the alternate bedroom floors of timber to reduce the total weight.

Denys Lasdun, Keeling House cluster block, Bethnal Green, London, 1958. Seen from Canrobert Street, the towers rise above the Victorian terraces that it was attempting to replicate vertically.

The access decks connecting to the service core helped to tie the cluster together and prevent horizontal movement. The structure was, like many concrete buildings of the period, a mixture of pre-cast elements and in situ casting which allowed for a relatively swift build time. The result is distinctive, and yet, like Sulkin House on Usk Street, of a human scale. This was achieved by placing pre-cast cruciform beams between the balconies to accentuate each maisonette dwelling, the basic two-up and two-down arrangement that reflected the Victorian terraces around it. Looking at it today, over fifty years on, it is easy to forget that Lasdun invested great effort in designing this block in sympathy with both the pre-exiting geography and the needs of the brief.

What we see at Keeling House is the burgeoning interest in strata that Lasdun would later employ to great effect at the University of East Anglia. This element of his design vocabulary becomes more apparent in a residential block he designed in St James's Place, overlooking Green Park and only a stone's throw from the Smithson's Economist Building. Being designed to meet the needs of an entirely different demographic gave Lasdun the opportunity to explore what could be achieved with the best materials and finishes. Because the block was designed for luxury above efficiency there was greater freedom in making use of the space available; where there are seven dwellings at St James's Place, approximately the same amount of space at Keeling House provided nearly twice as many.

Looking at the building from the Green Park side it may at first seem incongruous, sited as it is next to the Palladian Spencer House. But the scale is balanced by Spencer's other neighbour to the south, Charles Barry's Bridgewater House of 1846, which mirrors Lasdun's block in terms of height and also in the horizontal bands that delineate each floor. Lasdun's block has a visceral quality, the internal structure made visible on the exterior with pronounced overhangs on each floor, the cantilevered balconies and the undulation of the windows on the Green Park elevations.

The site on the edge of Green Park, just to the south of the Ritz Hotel, was originally occupied by two Georgian houses that were destroyed during the war. Lasdun's new block provided five large and three smaller apartments, including a penthouse with its own roof garden, designing the accommodation with a number of factors in mind: the views over Green Park, the provision of good-sized living rooms and also how the accommodation might change over time. This last element was achieved by arranging the service ducts, lighting and heating in a way that would allow for internal changes, the only inflexible element being the bathrooms and kitchens. In addition to all this, Lasdun took pains to ensure privacy and the minimum of noise by using anti-vibration bases for mechanical equipment, acoustic felt and baffles on all the ducting, double-glazed windows and fibre-glass quilting between the floors.

Convection heaters built into the window layout provided warmth for the apartments, the temperature in each room being independently variable by thermostat; to keep the heat in during the winter the walls were lined with cork and the bronze window frames were filled with expanding polystyrene. During the summer months the interior spaces were shielded by the overhanging balconies which acted as brise-soleil.

The structure relied on the central lift and the staircase core for stability, with reinforced concrete columns supporting in situ floor slabs, with edge beams holding up the cantilevered balconies. The exterior was clad in a mixture of materials, including grey granite, the soffits decorated with white ceramic mosaic and, to keep the exterior lines as free from unnecessary clutter as possible, rainwater gutters were concealed on each floor. The end result is a stunning piece of architecture, with great thought being applied to the quality of materials and efficiency of design. It was well received in its day, the Architectural Review stating succinctly that '... this is, quite simply, good architecture'. At St James's Place we see how the Brutalist aesthetic could not only be tolerated as a style to live with but became in this building one to admire and aspire to.

Denys Lasdun, Flats in St James's Place, London, 1958, seen from Green Park. On a more human scale and using materials and finishes designed for luxury and space.

Denys Lasdun, Flats in St James's Place, London, 1958. Nestling amid neo-classical structures the block is able to match its neighbours in terms of scale while remaining modern and, like his Charles Wilson building at Leicester University, showing strong horizontal forms in the design.

Park Hill

In the 1950s, the Sheffield Corporation Architects' Department developed a housing scheme at Park Hill that was to become the closest embodiment to date of the new ideas in social housing coursing through the debate in the architectural profession, the CIAM and Team 10. Ostensibly an imposing slab block of concrete construction, it is a considered design that seems elegantly to solve the problems of both a difficult site and a complex issue.

Chief architect John Lewis Womersley engaged Jack Lynn and Ivor Smith, and began work designing the project in 1953. The Park Hill area had been occupied by a traditional grid of terraced streets and in the pre-war era had become notorious for poverty, crime and violence. Attempts had been made to clear some of the site and rebuild, but following the war it became evident that a more radical approach was called for. The site itself was geographically challenging, being basically triangular in form and on a steep 1 in 10 incline. Womersley's solution was essentially a single, apparently meandering, block that maintains a level roofline while the number of floors changes to accommodate the hilly terrain, rising to fourteen at the lowest point and reducing to four storeys at the highest.

Seen from above, the Park Hill project can be viewed as four interconnecting arms of canted or hooked form, united by access bridges that coincide with street decks running the length of the whole scheme. It is these street decks that are of particular note. They are the expression of an idea espoused by Le Corbusier, realised internally in his *Unité d'Habitation* and conceived here externally, although within the skeleton of the blocks and so still affording shelter. Wide enough at 3m (10ft) to accommodate furniture removal and delivery vans, milk floats and small service vehicles, as well as children's play, the street decks run in uninterrupted linear promenades so that one can

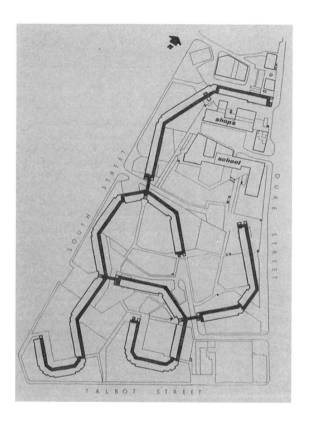

TOP: *Lewis Womersley with Sheffield Corporation Architects' Department, Park Hill Housing, Sheffield, 1961. Site plan.*

BOTTOM: *Lewis Womersley with Sheffield Corporation Architects' Department, Park Hill Housing, Sheffield, 1961. Section showing arrangement of dwellings.*

PREVIOUS PAGE: *Lewis Womersley with Sheffield Corporation Architects' Department, Park Hill Housing, Sheffield, 1961. South Street elevation.*

walk the entire length of the building without having to traverse up and down stairs. And because the arms of the block are of loosely curved form, the access elevations switch from one side to the other, with the deck cutting through at the end of a section, meaning that views from the dwellings do not all face the same way.

In the original construction, the decks accessed flats and maisonettes arranged in clusters, each accommodating two flats and two maisonettes arranged around a load-bearing H-form frame containing stair columns. All the kitchens and bathrooms were aligned vertically to allow the installation of simple ducting for services and waste disposal. This arrangement was repeated every three bays and the street decks every three floors with access to flats on the floor below and maisonettes on the same floor and the next above. While the idea of 'streets in the sky' was appealing to the architectural profession and critics alike, it was felt in some quarters that they lacked the opportunity for community and neighbourly interaction that a traditional terraced street might afford. This was partly because the only thing facing onto the decks was the front door of each flat, and also because no dwellings looked back from the other side, so to speak.

Construction of the scheme was a concrete frame, left exposed and unadorned, with brick infill of differing colours, including red, terracotta and cream. The use of these contrasting materials was influenced by the advice of consultant artist John Forrester, whose other touches included Mondrianesque screens by the lift access. Viewed from the outside, the overall aesthetic is massive and formidable, likened at the time to a fortified city wall. But the facades carry a good deal of incident with the geometric arrangement of balconies, windows and access decks. The influence of Le Corbusier is undeniable, partly in the realisation of the oft-mentioned street decks but also in the superficial similarities between the blocks at Park Hill and the *Unité d'Habitation*. But this was coincidental. Design of the scheme at Sheffield began in the year the *Unité* in Marseille was completed, and its architects were less concerned with outward appearances and instead happy to let the exterior be dictated by the arrangement of dwellings within. What Womersley and his team created at Park Hill was a considered and practical solution to large-scale urban living, doubling the capacity of the site, and incorporating a sensitivity to the community occupying it.

Lewis Womersley with Sheffield Corporation Architects' Department, Park Hill Housing, Sheffield, 1961. South Street elevation from the Granville Street footbridge.

Ernö Goldfinger

When one thinks of Brutalist architecture, the images conjured up are of heavy concrete volumes, rough-cast and starkly modern; the building that perhaps most closely resembles this picture is Trellick Tower by Ernö Goldfinger, completed in

1972. Indeed, this building more than any other has come to symbolize the Brutalist epoch, achieving iconic status, and has been cited, contrarily, by both sides of the argument for and against such architecture. Images of this building have been printed on t-shirts and mugs and its near identical sister site, Balfron Tower in Poplar, was used as the location for Danny Boyle's 2002 dystopian

Ernö Goldfinger, Balfron Tower, Poplar, London, 1968. The archetypal Massive Brutalist slab block with its separated lift and service tower, joined to the main block by enclosed walkways on alternate floors.

Ernö Goldfinger, Balfron Tower, Poplar, London, 1968. The scale is monumental and the materials reflect the spirit of the age, being modern, unadorned and rough-cast.

Ernö Goldfinger, Glenkerry House, Poplar, London, 1968. Here the service tower is joined to the main building and this smaller block carries motifs from its larger brother to remain aesthetically consistent.

Ernö Goldfinger, Carradale House, Poplar, London, 1968, view with Balfron Tower visible behind. Here the service tower bridges two low-rise blocks forming an 'L' shape.

science-fiction movie *28 Days Later*, starring Cillian Murphy, and is also thought to have been the inspiration for J.G. Ballard's novel *High Rise*. Such is the power of architecture to inspire, to foster strong emotions both positive and negative and to impress itself upon our consciousness and our culture.

Goldfinger's work in Britain gained the most momentum in the post-war years and the 1940s brought commissions for primarily commercial structures which, while showing stylistic elements of his later work, were rooted in the pre-war International Style. The first real precedent

for Trellick was the development at Elephant and Castle, including Alexander Fleming House, where we see design elements that would become Goldfinger trademarks: the expression of interior volumes on the exterior, the use of recessed bays, the undulating surface and separate service towers linked by glazed bridges.

Before Trellick Tower was built, though, Goldfinger won a commission to build a housing development at Rowlet Street in Poplar, close to the entrance of the Blackwall Tunnel. Completed in 1971, the development included three principle blocks: Carradale House, Glenkerry House and

Balfron Tower. It was the last of these that acted as a precursor to Trellick Tower, its layout and basic shape being almost identical, although on a slightly smaller scale. What Goldfinger was able to do here was put into practice the kind of social housing theories espoused by Le Corbusier in his work on the Ville Radieuse, with slab blocks arranged around open spaces. He also took details from the Unité d'Habitation and worked them into the structures; this is most readily visible on Balfron Tower, but even more so on the later Trellick, which almost appears like a sliver cut out of the Marseille block.

Ernö Goldfinger, Carradale House, Poplar, London, 1968. The surfaces are rough and brutal but softened with curved edges creating plasticity of form and interplay of light around the volumes.

The Rowlet Street development set the template with the headlining Balfron Tower standing on the eastern side with Carradale House set at a right angle to the north. The layout of Balfron included the main slab apartment block with a separate service, staircase and lift tower joined to it by glazed bridges at every third floor. The service tower also contained a rubbish chute and, at the top, the boiler room. The structure was largely in situ concrete, which Goldfinger trusted more for its structural strength than pre-cast elements, especially for higher-rise buildings.

At twenty-seven storeys, Balfron Tower was, when opened, the tallest housing block in Europe and almost immediately opinions were divided as to whether this marked a brave future for housing or the worst kind of architecture imaginable. So convinced was Goldfinger of the virtues of his work that he and his wife Ursula moved from their home in Willow Road to live for two months in Balfron Tower, taking an apartment on the twenty-sixth floor. In addition to experiencing the good and the bad of his building first-hand, Goldfinger was able to gain valuable insight that would help him to develop the next tower across London on Golbourne Road.

Trellick Tower was completed in 1972 as part of the Cheltenham Estate in north Kensington and, at thirty-one storeys, managed to pip Balfron Tower to the tallest apartment block in Europe accolade. Like its sister in Tower Hamlets, Trellick had the separate service tower with stairs, lifts and refuse chute as well as boiler room at the top. The internal structure with access decks and segments of double-height maisonettes is clearly visible from the outside and this resonates back again to Le Corbusier's Unité d'Habitation. The building contained nine different apartment types, all extending through the building with windows on both sides, and Goldfinger took pains to provide soundproofing as well as efficient heating and lighting in the well-proportioned rooms.

Both estates experienced service failures, poor management and vandalism almost from the outset, and these issues blighted a set of buildings which presented something new and

Ernö Goldfinger, Trellick Tower, Kensington, London, 1972. The big daddy of Brutalist tower bocks, following the form of Balfron Tower but incorporating design elements derived from the experiences of residents at its earlier cousin in Poplar.

Ernö Goldfinger, Trellick Tower, Kensington, London, 1972. The service tower with its curious glazed carbuncle at the top borrowed from Glenkerry House.

exciting in social housing in a way that was considered to be well designed and had the interests of its tenants at heart. They were also some of the most extraordinary and arresting structures in London, if not Britain, and still remain so. The surface textures and arrangement of volumes captured the spirit of Modernism in its current form, espoused by the rhetoric of Team 10, the CIAM splinter group which championed a new wave in heroic architecture.

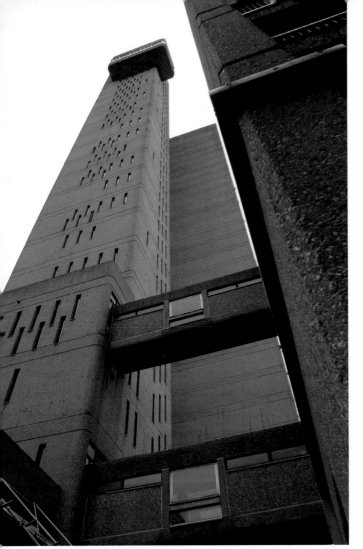

Housing formed an increasingly important part of the Smithsons' architectural direction and became central to their break with the rationalism of the CIAM in the 1950s, the basis of which was Le Corbusier's notion of keeping a balanced mixture of urban building functions: dwelling, work, recreation and transportation. What the Smithsons developed was rooted in the dwelling as the keystone to a wider context of streets within districts within cities. An important association for them at this time was with the photographer Nigel Henderson, whose images of street life in Bethnal Green inspired them to recreate these

Ernö Goldfinger, Trellick Tower, Kensington, London, 1972. The main tower linked to a low-rise block set at a right angle with enclosed bridges between. The fine grain aggregate seen at close quarters gives the whole scheme a uniform texture which has weathered consistently since completion.

The Smithsons

Two of the most active members of Team 10, Alison and Peter Smithson, had been busy while Goldfinger's buildings were hitting the skyline, with their own estate close to Balfron Tower in Poplar. Though much lower in height, the Robin Hood Gardens development was no less powerful a statement, a giant, meandering, concrete megastructure bristling with surface texture.

communities within high-rise developments. To do this they suggested long serpentine blocks with wide access galleries forming stacked terraces, designed to encourage interaction between tenants in the same way as occurred within the Victorian streets of the inner cities.

Their project proposal for Golden Lane in central London of 1952 clearly shows how they visualized a large, snaking, high-density block to work within the bomb-damaged city confines. This scheme was opposed to the Ville Radieuse model, with its slab blocks arranged in a grid form around open public spaces since what the Smithsons wanted

to achieve was intended to maintain community dynamics rather than to replace them with something entirely different. However, what they had not expected, as Kenneth Frampton pointed out in his book Modern Architecture, a Critical History (Thames & Hudson, 1985), was that three principal features of the by-law street would be absent in their proposed blocks: first, the dynamics

Alison and Peter Smithson, Robin Hood Gardens estate, Poplar, London, 1972. The realization of their response to mass housing which began with their Golden Lane proposal, a true Brutalist megastructure.

associated with dwellings on both sides of a street, secondly, the community life associated with the street at ground level, and, thirdly, the 'backyard' which played a crucial role in by-law housing and the life of its communities.

Alison and Peter Smithson continued their own work on perfecting this social housing type and one of the biggest commissions they received was for a new estate at Poplar in the district of Tower Hamlets. The solution was to create two serpentine slabs containing 200 dwellings and accessed by long, wide galleries, the blocks enclosing a central open space protected from the roads and laid to lawn with an artificial hillock in the centre and

John Wood the Younger, The Royal Crescent, Bath, 1767–74. At the apex of neo-classical design, elegant and perfectly proportioned.

Alison and Peter Smithson, Robin Hood Gardens estate, Poplar, London, 1972. The sweep of the slab blocks and their vertical texturing was designed to imitate the great curved terraces of the Georgian era.

a children's play area. The facades expressed the spaces within by a series of vertical fins attached, punctuated every so often by the stairway sections. From the outside, the fins play a lesser role to the more dominant, horizontal accents of the access galleries. The sweeping curves seen from within the courtyard are highly reminiscent of the royal crescents at Bath, and such comparisons have been made more than once by critics and historians studying this building.

What the Smithsons did at Poplar was to give life to their theories of concentrated housing schemes for the working classes in a region that was very much home ground to them. The style of architecture, which was uncompromisingly Modernist, did have its roots in classical proportions and served the dual function of acting as a foil to the much lauded point block, as well as expressing the mood of the day. It encapsulated the Brutalist ethic and aesthetic, like a giant Paolozzi sculpture for living in. But the practicalities of living in a work of art soon showed their shortcomings; the access galleries, while wide, did nothing to engender a community spirit as was visualized, the communal stairs and parking areas were prone to vandalism and petty crime, and the balconies were too small to be of much use beyond the ornamental.

ABOVE: Alison and Peter Smithson, Robin Hood Gardens estate, Poplar, London, 1972. The flats are accessed by decks on the exterior elevations while on the interior, facing the communal green, are the balconies.

RIGHT: Alison and Peter Smithson, Robin Hood Gardens estate, Poplar, London, 1972. With its canted corners and vertical emphasis there are parallels with the Economist building, but here rough-cast concrete predominates.

And yet other schemes which employed an aesthetic no less brutal built in other parts of London fared much better. Completed in the same year as Robin Hood Gardens, Patrick Hodgkinson's Brunswick Centre in Bloomsbury was a much more successful mixed-function, concrete megastructure. Here again, we find an alternative to the tower block but handled in a different way from the Smithsons'. The Brunswick Centre was constructed as two rows of stepped terraces, the ziggurat form recalling quite strongly Lasdun's University of East Anglia. On the upper levels were the apartments, elevated above a wide precinct with shops, offices and a cinema.

Hodgkinson had studied housing types with Leslie Martin, with particular reference to the LCC's Loughborough Road estate, a series of slab blocks highly reminiscent of the Unité d'Habitation, to establish whether low-rise, high-density housing was a viable alternative. The opportunity to put these theories and calculations to the test came in 1959 when Marchmont Properties commissioned Hodgkinson and Martin to design a scheme on a site then owned by the Foundling Hospital. In its early stages, as negotiations began with the LCC the scheme was known as 'The Foundling Project' and after the proposals had been reviewed and adapted, construction eventually began in 1968.

Patrick Hodgkinson, The Brunswick Centre, Bloomsbury, London, 1972. The central plaza with shop fronts and restaurants at ground level and residential blocks terraced above.

With the guidance of McAlpine as engineering consultants, as well as financial backers of the project, the construction was of mixed materials with brick, reinforced concrete and rendered blockwork. The completed structure comprised two long, low blocks with stepped horizontal accents, punctuated with Lasdunesque service towers; that on the Marchmont Street side of ziggurat form while opposing this on the Brunswick Square side of diagonal shape supported by a framework of concrete fin-like buttresses. The 560 apartments were of one- or two-bedroom flat and maisonette type, all single aspect with glass-covered balconies. Beneath them are the rows of shops facing into the precinct and below this elevated plaza a subterranean car park with spaces for over 900 vehicles.

Patrick Hodgkinson, The Brunswick Centre, Bloomsbury, London, 1972, Marchmont Street elevation showing the residential terraces with glazed enclosed balconies.

Patrick Hodgkinson, The Brunswick Centre, Bloomsbury, London, 1972. Supporting the outward sweeping access decks on the Brunswick Square elevation are a series of flying buttresses.

Patrick Hodgkinson, The Brunswick Centre, Bloomsbury, London, 1972. The 'Lasdunesque' service towers rise above the roof line and add colour and vertical texture.

Patrick Hodgkinson, The Brunswick Centre, Bloomsbury, London, 1972. On the Brunswick Square elevation with Renoir cinema nestled between residential blocks and a walkway through to the plaza.

Low-rise Schemes

A housing scheme, which bears some superficial resemblance to the Brunswick Centre and employed the same twin facing, low-rise terraced blocks, with central precinct format, was the Alexandra Road development at Swiss Cottage, completed in 1978, designed by Neave Brown and the Camden Architects Department and, like its Bloomsbury counterpart, one that can be seen as another of the more successful Transitional Brutalist megastructures.

The low-rise scheme had become well established as a counterpoint to tower blocks, which had, by the late 1960s, suffered from the blights of poor maintenance and vandalism. High-rise building had also been greatly diluted by so-called LPS or 'large panel system' building, using pre-fabricated, concrete construction, concerning the like of which Goldfinger had already expressed serious doubts. The structural shortcomings of system-building became all too clear when, in 1968, a gas explosion on the eighteenth floor of Ronan Point, a prefab, twenty-three-storey block in Newham, East London, caused a catastrophic collapse of the whole south-east corner from top to bottom, killing four people. The disaster happened barely two months after the building had been completed and, even though Ronan Point was rebuilt, this episode caused irreparable damage to the concept of high-rise living in Britain. Even though much better built schemes, such as those of Goldfinger and Lasdun, would outlive system-built blocks, they were tarred with the same brush and considered, quite wrongly, equally suspect.

And so the low-rise developments that had been constructed in some London boroughs with much less debate than in the era of the tower block, such as Darbourne and Darke's Lillington Gardens in Pimlico and Neave Brown's Dunboyne Road estate in Camden, began to emerge as the logical and most viable alternative in the mass-housing stakes. While they did put down a much larger footprint than the average point block, the notion of high-density schemes on a more human scale was firmly rooted in the Georgian terrace and so had a workable precedent on which it could be based.

Alexandra Road was designed to provide housing in an area of land bordered to one side by railway tracks, and to do so in such a way as to make use of the site without allowing intrusion from noise and vibration. The solution was to build three rows of terraced apartments and maisonettes, the first on the north side adjacent to the tracks of eight storeys in reinforced concrete, the back of which were cantilevered with vertical ribs to bounce the noise back and shelter the single-aspect dwellings on its front elevation. Opposing this across a public walkway was the second, lower block of four storeys. These two rows follow a gentle curve, and, looking west, down this V-shaped valley of concrete, the similarity to the Brunswick Centre is quite apparent. The south elevation of the second four-storey block has garden-aspect dwellings which face a public park, gently rising up to the third terrace. In situ concrete was used throughout, which pushed the cost of the project well above budget, a factor that brought the estate some criticism but which now can be seen as contributing to its longevity, the quality of materials and the finish clearly making a difference to the tenants and local authority who have maintained it well.

PREVIOUS PAGE: Camden Borough Council (Neave Brown), Alexandra Road Estate, Swiss Cottage, London, 1978. The brick paved 'street' between the 'V' shape of maisonettes which gently sweeps following the path of the adjacent railway line.

Brown had experimented with the low-rise terrace in Winscombe Street with a row of five dwellings built for himself and friends in 1967. Though without much of the vigorous plastic form of the valley blocks at Alexandra Road, they bear a strong resemblance to the garden-aspect dwellings facing the park and can be seen as a precursor to his housing projects of the 1970s, as well as part of the transitional trend that was taking hold of this aspect of the industry. In the same year as Winscombe Street, the Architectural Review published an article by Nicholas Taylor entitled 'The Failure of Housing', in which he studied the way in which the basic standards required of housing have changed and evolved since the nineteenth-century by-laws and, quite prophetically, how the demands made on the new housing stock of the day would change as society evolved. He cited the Parker Morris Report of 1961, Homes for Today and Tomorrow, which had indicated even then these rapidly changing needs:

> … the increasing independence of the teenager, the increasing homework of the student, the increasing mechanical equipment of the housewife, the increasing storage of the family's leisure wear and leisure gear. All of these, note, are increasing, and what is here and now acceptable to middle-aged refugees from the back-to-back may well seem derisory to their children and grandchildren.

Taylor also noted that the physical decay of Brutalist housing estates was rapid, and, while the objective shortcomings of the structures could easily be defined, what could not was the subjective 'hatred' of these rough-cast concrete buildings by their tenants. Much later in the *Architects' Journal* of 1999, Paul Hyett in his article on Trellick Tower suggested that many of the problems associated with the high-rise social housing of the East End were not entirely the fault of their design and that many of the issues that blighted them would evaporate if they were emptied of their tenants and relocated wholesale to an upmarket Regent's Park address.

Camden Borough Council (Neave Brown), Alexandra Road Estate, Swiss Cottage, London, 1978. The rear elevation of the south block bordering parkland with more conventional terraced gardens.

Camden Borough Council (Neave Brown), Alexandra Road Estate, Swiss Cottage, London, 1978. The concrete megastructure of the North block is raised above ground level with parking bays and road access below.

This theory need not be put to the test as an example exists in reality in the form of the Barbican complex by Chamberlin, Powell and Bon, completed in 1981, studied in more detail in the previous chapter. Here, nestled close to the capital's financial district, is a quiet, well-maintained and pleasant environment to live in, free from vandalism and comparatively free from crime, and yet no less brutal in aesthetics than either Trellick Tower or, indeed, Robin Hood Gardens.

Camden Borough Council (Neave Brown), Alexandra Road Estate, Swiss Cottage, London, 1978. A view between blocks on the South side facing North showing the strata of dwellings with access stairs at intervals, the units clearly articulated with projecting floor and wall slabs.

OTHER NOTABLE BRUTALIST HOUSING SCHEMES

Alton East Housing Estate, Roehampton (LCC Architects' Department, 1959): a series of Corbusian slab blocks resembling the *Unité d'Habitation,* arranged on a gently undulating site. It seemed to encapsulate, although on a smaller scale to the *Unité,* Le Corbusier's vision of town planning.

Point Royal Flats, Bracknell, Berkshire (Arup Associates, 1964): a point block based on hexagonal geometry, the flats arranged around a central service core, the whole block cantilevered over a recessed entrance foyer.

Lillington Gardens, Lillington Street, London (Darbourne and Darke, 1972): a high-density scheme on a more human scale than Robin Hood, utilizing low-rise structures combining brick and concrete to soften its profile and blend with the surrounding buildings.

World's End Housing, Cheyne Walk, London (Eric Lyons, Cadbury-Brown, Metcalfe and Cunningham, 1977): transitional use of brick in a series of highly sculptural tower blocks and low-rise clusters.

Chapter 7

Ecclesiastical Building

Although some saw the post-war period as one where old traditions would be swept aside, the wider public in Britain had not turned its back on the church. Far from it, in fact, and so the several faiths had work to do in order to accommodate a growing congregation. Some dioceses had to rebuild bomb-damaged chapels and cathedrals. Others commissioned entirely new buildings on sites where previously there had been none. Changes in the shape of ecclesiastical building had already happened on the Continent and so, in the spirit of rebirth, British faiths turned to Modernist architects to break with the traditional forms of Gothic and Neo-classical and the old internal templates. The same elements would be there, but arranged in a way that sought to blend more readily with the way congregations use them and flow through them. This, in essence, was the new liturgical movement which had gained momentum in France after the building of Le Corbusier's Notre Dame du Haut chapel at Ronchamp.

Cathedral building immediately after the Second World War began, though, with the Indian summer of traditional form lingering on, most notably at Liverpool with Giles Scott's Anglican Cathedral, construction of which had begun in 1904 and was still being completed in the 1960s, and with Edward Maufe's Guildford Cathedral, begun in 1936 and then completed between 1952 and 1965. In these two buildings one can see the beginnings of a transition from the resolutely historicist towards a Modernist style. They are of roughly similar shape and proportions, but the Gothic detail in Scott's work is stripped down into simple, stylized forms in Maufe's. At Guildford one can see the arrangement of volumes without distraction, and it has an almost industrial simplicity, rather reminiscent of Behrens's Turbine Factory, except for the tower.

The foundations had been laid for more challenging and exciting structures that captured the spirit of the twentieth century while remaining true to the functions of a modernizing church, without overt references to the architecture of ancient Greece and Rome or medieval Britain.

Coventry

One of the earliest major commissions of the post-war period was Coventry Cathedral. The city had been one of the more heavily bombarded during the blitz and a casualty of this had been the original Perpendicular cathedral which was destroyed in November 1940. What survived was a shell of the exterior walls, and, miraculously, its tower and spire, considered to be among the finest in England. After some lengthy discussions, the design of a new cathedral was laid open to competition in 1951. Out of more than 200 shortlisted entrants the design of Basil Spence was chosen, the only one to include and incorporate the ruins of the original building.

Essentially Spence's Coventry was a basilica form with two circular side chapels, Unity and Industry, attached to the entrance and apse ends on opposite sides of the building. Linking the new and the old cathedral was a high canopy enclosing a massive glass screen. From the apse the new building rose upward to meet the old, ramping up to remain in scale with the tower and spire. The side walls were of sawtooth form, inset with stained-glass, vertical windows from floor to ceiling which transmitted graduated light down the nave towards the apse and the high altar.

The exterior was clad in red sandstone from Hollington in Staffordshire, which remained in keeping with local materials and colours, Spence once again taking great pains to integrate his new building with its wider setting. The entrance canopy was made accessible from both east and west and it is on the eastern side that one encounters the first piece of commissioned art, Jacob Epstein's sculpture of St Michael and Lucifer. Also on this side is the rounded form of the massive baptistry window with its geometric tracery.

PREVIOUS PAGE: *Sir Basil Spence, Coventry Cathedral, 1962. East elevation with 'sawtooth' walls inset with stained glass and the entrance canopy bridging the new with the old bomb-damaged building. (Image courtesy of Tim Eccleston and Coventry Cathedral)*

OPPOSITE: *Sir Basil Spence, Coventry Cathedral, 1962. The nave with narrow tapering columns, rib-vaulted ceiling and tapestry by Graham Sutherland. (Image courtesy of Tim Eccleston and Coventry Cathedral)*

ABOVE RIGHT: *Sir Basil Spence, Coventry Cathedral, 1962. The entrance canopy with access to the Baptistry and beyond as well as the original Gothic cathedral and tower. (Image courtesy of Tim Eccleston and Coventry Cathedral)*

RIGHT: *Sir Basil Spence, Coventry Cathedral, 1962. Facing South and looking through the huge glass screen with etched angels and saints by John Hutton. (Image courtesy of Tim Eccleston and Coventry Cathedral)*

Sir Basil Spence, Coventry Cathedral 1962. The visceral metal of Jacob Epstein's St.Michael and Lucifer set against the soft pink of the stone. (Image courtesy of Tim Eccleston and Coventry Cathedral)

Sir Basil Spence, Coventry Cathedral, 1962. Inside the Chapel of Unity with its slightly tapering cylindrical form, exposed concrete walls and narrow vertical stained-glass windows. (Image courtesy of Tim Eccleston and Coventry Cathedral)

Once inside, the visitor is confronted with a huge glass screen engraved with angels and saints by John Hutton. Beyond this was the baptistry with its font fairly dwarfed by the massive window bay, and then the nave and aisles laid out in a traditional form leading to the high altar. The lofty ceiling is decorated with a web of rib vaulting formed from reinforced concrete with wood slatting between, supported by two rows of cruciform columns which taper slightly towards the base. The interior was originally intended to be faced in pink stone, but, instead, was left in its pale grey, rough-cast concrete finish, partly for economy but also to allow a more effective transmission of light from the windows.

Apart from the architect's flair for combining materials and finishes to unrivalled quality, on this project he assembled a team of commissioned artists and designers to work on specific features of the interior. The practitioners were selected by Spence regardless of age, experience or reputation, but on his own instinct and knowledge of their work, matching incredibly well the skills needed for each required task. This process was crucial to Spence's project and the nature of his design, forming an inexorable bond between the building and the art within it. In addition to Epstein's entrance sculpture and Hutton's screen there was a tapestry hanging behind the high altar by Graham Sutherland, depicting Christ in a way faintly reminiscent of the Turin shroud, the stained-glass windows of the baptistry were by John Piper and Patrick Reyntiens, while that of the zigzag walls was by students of the Royal College of Art. Tablets of stone placed on the interior walls were carved with inscriptions by Ralph Beyer, as was the inscription on the altar roundel in the Chapel of Industry. Throughout the building other works and details by Geoffrey Clarke, Lawrence Lee, Hans Coper, Steven Sykes and Keith New combine to create an experience of drama, a spiritual journey that had been carefully stage-managed by Spence and his team.

This was an important building, not just for Coventry but for Britain as a whole. It symbolized so many things, the regeneration of a society scarred by war, the rebuilding of towns and cities from the rubble of the blitz, the revival of Britain's churches and faiths and, in no small way, the reinvigoration of the architectural profession in this country. For all these reasons there was a microscope poised over Coventry and this must have exerted great pressure on Spence. A lesser architect might not have coped as well, but Spence managed to work without compromising his values, in close consultation with the diocese and his team of artists and designers.

The result, consecrated in 1962, was almost universally applauded and earned its architect a knighthood among many other accolades. The conspicuous voices of dissent came from the avant-garde and so one must question whether Coventry Cathedral was a truly Modernist and, indeed, a Brutalist building. Clearly, Spence drew much influence from the original cathedral in terms of exterior materials and the many Gothic references in the design. Just as clearly this was not the heavy massing of concrete volumes as would later be found at Queen Anne's Gate or Salters' Hall. But what we do have at Coventry is something commanding, bold and very much of its time. There are asymmetrical volumes, there is unadorned concrete. If it is Brutalism it is of the Early variety found in the immediate post-war years, but, even so, one can see elements that would appear in Spence's later work from the Massive and the Transitional period. It also set the pace for Modernist ecclesiastical building and a high watermark for other architects to aim at over the succeeding two decades and beyond.

In 1959 Frederick Gibberd was commissioned to design a chapel at Hopwood Hall in Middleton, Manchester, for De La Salle Teacher Training College. The design was striking, a tapering tower above a polygonal, chamfered rotunda. It was largely brick-built, with pre-cast concrete spines forming the tower and was a design that Gibberd would enlarge upon at Liverpool, with his iconic Metropolitan Cathedral completed in 1967.

Liverpool

The siting of a new Roman Catholic cathedral at Brownlow Hill was a project launched in 1929 under the leadership of the then Archbishop of Liverpool Dr Richard Downey. The original commission was awarded to Sir Edwin Lutyens after a chance meeting between the architect and Downey at the Garrick Club the same year. The Metropolitan Cathedral of Christ the King would sit at the opposite end of Hope Street to Giles Scott's Anglican Cathedral and Lutyens's design would rise above the city, a mighty Byzantine structure with what would have been the largest dome in Europe. Lutyens's estimate for the project in 1930 was £3,000,000 and, once the site had been cleared and his plans blessed by Pope Pius XI, work began with the crypt. The Second World War intervened and building was suspended, although Lutyens continued to work on the design. In spite of the architect's death in 1944, the project continued but the estimated costs began to spiral and by 1953 had reached £17,000,000 and so Lutyens's grand scheme had to be abandoned with only the crypt itself having been completed.

In 1959 a competition was launched to re-design the Metropolitan Cathedral with, among other stipulations, a brief to incorporate the crypt in the design. Judged by Archbishop Heenan, David Stokes and Basil Spence, the 293 proposals were gradually whittled down to that of Frederick Gibberd.

His extraordinary building is one of the most distinctive and recognizable structures in Britain; likened to a wigwam or a giant shuttlecock, it presents a diametric contrast to its Anglican counterpart and has become as much a symbol of the city itself as the Royal Liver Building and its attendant birds. Gibberd's original design had an exterior profile much more like that of Hopwood Hall chapel, but the structural engineers on the project, Lowe and Rodin, recommended flying buttresses which would extend down from the roof cone to provide necessary additional support. Gibberd himself was not keen on the way these altered the appearance of the building and he feared that it would seem to some observers to resemble Niemeyer's cathedral at Brasilia, at least superficially.

Gibberd used the footprint of Lutyens's basilica as the foundation for his plaza, with an open gathering space on the northern end above the crypt, leading to the geometric fantasy of the cathedral itself rising above the Blessed Sacrament chapel. On the Hope Street side are the main entrance porch and the bell tower, formed as two opposing and overlapping triangles. Beneath the roof

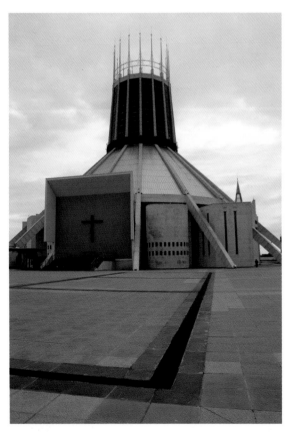

Frederick Gibberd, Liverpool Metropolitan Cathedral of Christ the King, Liverpool, 1967. The North elevation with plaza above Sir Edwin Lutyens crypt.

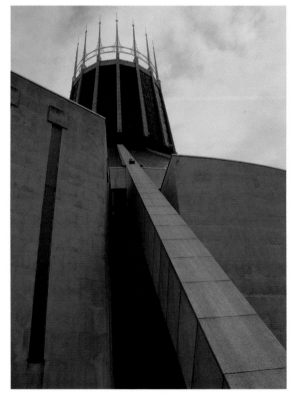

Frederick Gibberd, Liverpool Metropolitan Cathedral of Christ the King, Liverpool, 1967. The flying buttresses were not part of the original design but recommended by the project engineer, ultimately giving the cathedral its distinctive 'shuttlecock' shape.

canopy and nestling behind the guarding safety of the flying buttresses are fourteen subsidiary volumes, the side chapels, which help to give weight and grounding to the structure. Surmounting the conical roof is the tapering lantern with stained glass designed by John Piper and Patrick Reyntiens, the whole topped with a crown of steel spines. These serve, first, as a counterpoint to Scott's Anglican tower while also acting, as Gibberd put it, to help his tower dissolve into the surrounding geography.

One of the other key specifics of the brief, in addition to incorporating Lutyens' crypt, was the concept of the high altar being 'enshrined' by the cathedral rather than acting as an ornament within it. Gibberd's response to this was to place the altar in the centre, with the congregation

LEFT: *Frederick Gibberd, Liverpool Metropolitan Cathedral of Christ the King, Liverpool, 1967. The South entrance canopy with stonework by William Mitchell.*

BELOW: *Frederick Gibberd, Liverpool Metropolitan Cathedral of Christ the King, Liverpool, 1967, interior with central high altar surmounted by the aluminium tubular baldacchino.*

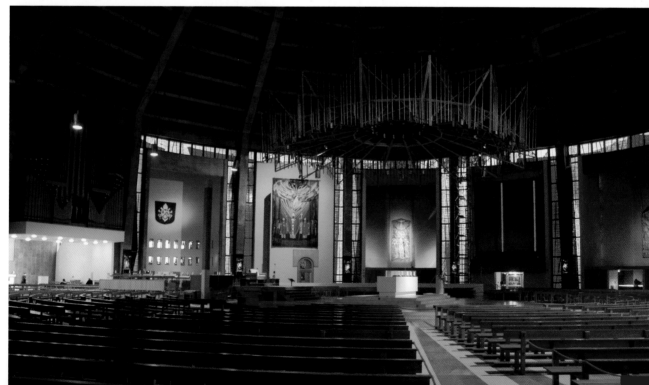

Frederick Gibberd, Liverpool Metropolitan Cathedral of Christ the King, Liverpool, 1967. The iconic central lantern by John Piper and Patrick Reyntiens supported on its concrete ring beam.

Frederick Gibberd, Liverpool Metropolitan Cathedral of Christ the King, Liverpool, 1967. The interior showing one of the fourteen side chapels amid exposed concrete beams and the ethereal hue of the stained-glass windows.

arranged around it on moveable, curved benches designed by Frank Height. Above the altar, and forming a link between it and the lantern, was a baldacchino constructed from aluminium tubing which was also designed and constructed to provide some artificial light, heating and ventilation. The individual side chapels were articulated with vivid blue, glass frames, also by Piper and Reyntiens, which provide an almost neon glow to the interior space.

Like many of the more significant structures of the period, a tremendous attention to detail was afforded the Metropolitan Cathedral. And here also the relationship between architecture and art was strong. Piper and Reyntiens's crowning glory in the lantern was constructed using 2.5cm (1in)-thick pieces of glass cemented together with epoxy resin and set into a unique tracery of narrow concrete ribs. The whole piece gave three bursts of light intended to represent the Holy Trinity against a graduated spectral background, and the whole piece weighed over 2,000 tonnes (1,960 tons). Other works of art included a sculpture of the Madonna by Bob Brumby, the reredos by Ceri Richards, the Hope Street entrance banner with crosses and crowns carved by William Mitchell, and the altar cross inside sculpted by Elizabeth Frink.

Cambridge

When Richard Sheppard won the competition to build Churchill College for Cambridge University (1961–64), beating Stirling and Gowan among others, part of his original plan included a chapel beside the main entrance. The very notion of a chapel for the college sparked an interesting debate which had, at its core, the essence of faith in post-war Britain and its place in society, as much as the liturgical revolution in building design for churches. There was considerable feeling among many Fellows of the College that a chapel had no place within a modern institution dedicated to scientific research and study.

Richard Sheppard, Chapel at Churchill College, Cambridge, 1967. The mix of brick and concrete soften the effect of an ambiguous assemblage of cuboid forms. (Image courtesy of Iqbal Alaam)

Inversely, there was equal weight to the argument that the College should have a chapel and would be incomplete without one. The debate reached such a pitch that Francis Crick, co-discoverer of the structure of DNA, resigned his fellowship, but, in spite of this, there was still the lingering notion that Christianity was inextricably bound up with life at Cambridge and that provision should be made for all colleges to at least offer some spiritual guidance.

Finally, a compromise was reached in 1967 by placing the chapel building in a far corner of the playing fields and referring to it as the Chapel at Churchill College rather than of Churchill College. Sheppard's scheme for the whole College was a work of great modernity and befitting the institution's primary mode of study. The architectural theme was a combination of brick and concrete and one can observe in many of the structures echoes once again of Le Corbusier's Maison Jaoul and, consequently, Spence's Sussex University. Indeed, Spence was one of the judges for Churchill College, along with Leslie Martin.

The chapel, however, seems to show influences from the Dutch inter-war De Stijl movement, with its assemblage of squares and rectangles like a cubist sculpture. The Cartesian coordinates that so inspired the De Stijl designers such as Piet Mondrian and Gerrit Rietveld are strongly present here in the bell tower and in the way the concrete canopy intersects the outer walls. In keeping with the liturgical movement, the chapel is of a Greek cross plan arranged around a central altar. The outer brick walls are intersected with vertical strip windows, with stained glass by John Piper.

Inside, the cruciform shape is accentuated by the massive concrete roof supports, lifted on four heavy, square-section, concrete columns. The roof itself is of timber with a central lantern beneath which hangs a giant, three-dimensional cross, again mirroring the De Stijl influence of its setting, designed by Keith Thyssen. The interior is cloistered, bathed in polychromatic hues from Piper's windows, and provides a small oasis of calm reflection.

Bristol

Ronald Weeks of the Percy Thomas Partnership was the chief architect for another influential Massive-period building, the Cathedral Church of SS Peter and Paul at Clifton Park in Bristol, completed in 1973, which, like its cousin in Liverpool, is one of the most impressive *avant-garde* ecclesiastical buildings in Britain. Its aggregate and concrete exterior rises up to a pinnacle like a crystalline outcrop, showing clear influences from early twentieth-century Expressionist architecture such as Bruno Taut's Steel Pavilion at Leipzig (1913). This theme continues on the inside where geometry abounds in the volumes, the massive wall and roof beams, and the central roof lantern.

Gibberd's Liverpool Cathedral, with its 'theatre in the round' layout in sympathy with the new liturgical movement, pre-empted Clifton, although the architects here seemed to work much more closely with the diocese, studying the flow of ceremonial movement and designing a building to work with these processes rather than focusing on the altar and then building around it.

The interior, with its Expressionist geometry, a stunning controlled use of light, careful placement of functional spaces and the quality of finish and materials, is very theatrical, almost cinematic. There is great drama here but also a welcoming atmosphere. It was clearly an important community space and Weeks managed to create something modern and stylized, but also of such high quality that it has been able to stand the passage of time to remain highly regarded and used today exactly as it was designed to. This emphasis on the quality of materials and finish, as well as care over design, is a key factor in the longevity of modern architecture and this is something that Weeks, like his contemporaries Spence and Lasdun, recognized and insisted upon.

As with the other influential ecclesiastical buildings of the period, there was a strong emphasis on commissioned art works at Clifton. William Mitchell designed the Stations of the Cross, while Henry Haig produced the stained-glass windows.

ABOVE: Richard Weeks (Percy Thomas Partnership), Clifton RC Cathedral, Bristol, 1973. The interior with high altar 'in the round' as befitting the new liturgical movement, the scale of the interior is dramatic with a strong geometry throughout. (Image courtesy of David Martyn)

OPPOSITE: Richard Weeks (Percy Thomas Partnership), Clifton RC Cathedral, Bristol, 1973. A starkly modern crystalline form with expressionist overtones and a high degree of quality and finish in the materials. (Image courtesy of David Martyn)

During the latter part of the twentieth century the new revolution in architecture could well have bypassed church building in Britain. The traditional forms found at Liverpool's Anglican Cathedral could have heralded a continuing momentum for Gothic and Neo-classical form had the country's dioceses not considered alternatives. The new liturgical movement, which is said to have begun at Bow Common in London with Maguire and Murray's St Paul's Church, led to the opening up of ecclesiastical building to the wider architectural profession and the grand, sometimes breathtaking, schemes of Spence and Gibberd set the mood for faiths that were increasing their congregations and were clearly keen to move with the times. The Brutalist aesthetic which, at least for Alison and Peter Smithson, spoke of the realities of urban life, could also be found to demonstrate sensitivity and spirituality as well as high drama.

OTHER NOTABLE BRUTALIST ECCLESIASTICAL BUILDINGS

Chapter Hall, Truro Cathedral, Cornwall (MWT Architects, 1967): like Scott's Guildhall extension, the Gothic detail of the cathedral is echoed in this chapter hall, a heavy cruciform deck raised on four square columns, with narrow vertical windows.

St Peter's College, Cardross, Scotland (Gillespie, Kidd and Coia, 1966): a Massive-period treatise in concrete construction, with interconnecting volumes, dramatic cantilevers, sculptural forms and brutal yet elegant geometry. Tragically unused and neglected today and in an advanced state of decay.

MWT Architects, Chapter Hall, Truro Cathedral, Cornwall, 1967. The use of slate and granite form links with local building traditions while remaining modern in form and incorporating Gothic detail to reflect the Victorian Cathedral. (Image courtesy of Darren Ashley)

Chapter 8

Conclusion and the Future of Brutalism

The recent past is just as worthy of respect as the distant past – and it needs it much more. We have a greater responsibility for modern buildings. We must hand them on to posterity untampered with.

Denys Lasdun, 1995

Brutalism was born and developed in an age of dramatic contradictions. While scientific discoveries heralded great advancements for the peoples of the world, they also provided the threat of its destruction in the form of a nuclear holocaust and pollution. While peace had been won in Europe, a cold war raged on ever harder. While international trade brought consumerism to the masses, the gap between rich and poor grew wider. The harsh realities of post-war Britain and the resonances it felt from the wider world found form culturally in the music of The Clash and The Sex Pistols, in the art of Francis Bacon and Eduardo Paolozzi and in the writings of Ray Bradbury and Anthony Burgess. British cinema audiences were exposed to many bleak visions of the future in motion pictures such as Franklin J. Schaffner's *Planet of the Apes (1968)* and George Lucas's *THX 1138* (1973). This brutalization of culture permeated through industrial design, and, of course, architecture and so shaped the way we lived, the way we worked and the way we viewed and reacted to the post-war world.

Brutalism was not, of course, the only form of architecture on the menu but it was a dominant form of Modernism in Britain through the 1950s, 1960s and 1970s, and it was Modernism that captured the mood and spirit of the age, that formed a pervasive part of the architectural profession and that won a large proportion of the commissions. But, as this book has explored the style in detail, it becomes clear that, as with pre-war Modernism, it was not a cohesive and single-minded movement. There were factions, such as Team 10, dedicated to keeping Modernism fresh and vital and tackling the important issues of the built environment. There were individual architects such as Basil Spence, Denys Lasdun and James Stirling who seemed to capture the essence of Brutalism in many of their works and yet actively sought to stand apart from those who referred to themselves as Brutalists.

What is also clear is that the term Brutalism is a style that, in Britain at least, managed to develop within it a broad range of materials and responses to briefs and sites. Rough-cast concrete, though more often than not an element of these buildings, was not always predominant. Other, more traditional materials, such as brick, stone and marble, were used to great effect while remaining convincingly modern. And many buildings were not thoughtless carbuncles which had been wedged into position amid much older Historicist buildings. More often than not, the architects took great pains to integrate their schemes with the site in terms of colour, texture, dimensions and stylistic elements.

British Modernist architecture of the post-war period has an uncertain future. Because its aesthetics have always been questioned and because some of it has either never worked as well as it was hoped or has, over time, become outgrown and obsolete, the Damoclean wrecking ball hangs threateningly above it. While many buildings have been protected with listed status some have not, and important examples could be lost forever. And heritage protection itself does not provide all the answers, as can be seen with Gillespie, Kidd and Coia's St Peter's College in Cardross, Argyll (1968), which has suffered terrible dilapidation since its listing in 1987. A great deal of effort must be exerted for any building to survive into the future in a form that can be used, studied and appreciated.

In spite of the debates about the aesthetic qualities of many period Brutalist buildings, the style has been revived in more recent years. This should come as no surprise as the nature of Post-modernism is to plunder styles of the past, recycle them, adapt them and mash them together. Neo-brutalism, therefore, has become part of the architectural scene in the twenty-first century and can be found in such buildings as Will Alsop's Peckham Public Library (2000) and Ian Simpson's Beetham Tower in Manchester (2006). But the use of concrete is now contentious as its production also yields 5 per cent of the world's carbon dioxide emissions, and so megastructures such as Robin Hood Gardens and East Anglia University are unlikely to be built in the future. But Brutalism is an adaptable style and other materials can easily be used, perhaps in this way finding a greater acceptance.

What is important for the future of Brutalism is that it is understood in the wider context of architectural history. It may not appeal to everyone and may not yet have the weight of antiquity behind it, but that does not mean, as Denys Lasdun said, that it deserves less respect than more ancient styles. By studying and understanding Brutalism, by appreciating its place in our past, in spite of its appearance, at least some Brutalist buildings may live on as physical examples for future students and architects to learn from.

Ernö Goldfinger, Trellick Tower, Kensington, London, 1972. Here the arrangement of balconies on the south elevation from Elkstone Road strongly echo Le Corbusier's Unite d'Habitation.

Bibliography

Books

Brooks Pfeiffer, Bruce, *Frank Lloyd Wright* (Taschen, 1991)

Curtis, William J.R., *Modern Architecture since 1900* (Phaidon, 1994)

Curtis, William J.R., *Denys Lasdun: Architecture, City, Landscape* (Phaidon, 1994)

Dean, David, *The 30s: Recalling the English Architectural Scene* (Trefoil Books, 1983)

Fleming, John, Hugh Honour and Nikolaus Pevsner, *The Penguin Dictionary of Architecture* (Penguin, 1980)

Frampton, Kenneth, *Modern Architecture, a Critical History* (Thames & Hudson, 1990)

Gould, Jeremy, *Modern Houses in Britain* (Society of Architectural Historians, 1977)

Hauffe, Thomas, *Design: a Concise History* (Laurence King, 1998)

Hitchcock, Henry Russell, *Architecture: Nineteenth and Twentieth Centuries* (Pelican History of Art, 1968)

Hughes, Quentin, *Liverpool: City of Architecture* (Bluecoat Press, 1999)

Jenger, Jean, *Le Corbusier: Architect of a New Age* (Thames & Hudson, 1996)

Long, Phillip and Jane Thomas (eds), *Basil Spence, Architect* (National Galleries of Scotland, 2008)

Lutyens, Mary, *Edwin Lutyens* (Black Swan, 1991)

Murray, Peter and Stephen Trombley (eds), *Modern British Architecture since 1945* (Frederick Muller and RIBA Magazines, 1984)

Overy, Paul, *De Stijl* (Thames & Hudson, 1991)

Powers, Alan, *Britain* (Reaktion Books, 2007)

Schildt, Goran, *Alvar Aalto: The Mature Years* (Rizzoli, 1991)

Winter, John, *Modern Buildings* (Paul Hamlyn, 1969)

Whitford, Frank, *Bauhaus* (Thames & Hudson, 1988)

Specialist Publications

The Architectural Review (Emap Ltd)
The Architects' Journal (Emap Ltd)
Building (United Business Media)
Building Design (United Business Media)
Concrete Quarterley (Concrete Centre)

Social Media

facebook.com/brutalist.architecture
Twitter: @Brutalism101
Instagram: @brutalism101

Index